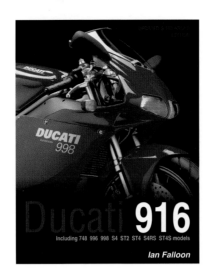

UPDATED & ENLARGED EDITION

DUCATI
998

Ducati **916**

Including 748 996 998 S4 ST2 ST4 S4RS ST4S models

Ian Falloon

Other great books from Veloce –

www.veloce.co.uk

First published in May 2017 by Veloce Publishing Limited, Veloce House, Parkway Farm Business Park, Middle Farm Way, Poundbury, Dorchester DT1 3AR, England. Fax 01305 250479 / e-mail info@veloce.co.uk / web www.veloce.co.uk or www.velocebooks.com. ISBN: 978-1-845849-42-9 UPC: 6-36847-04942-3

DUCATI

DUCATI
testastretta
998

Ducati **916**

Including 748 996 998 S4 ST4 S4RS ST4S models

Ian Falloon

Contents

Introduction and acknowledgements

There is no doubt that the 916, and its derivatives, were the most significant models ever produced by Ducati. The 916 single-handedly elevated the status of the company from that of a niche market producer of non-mainstream V-twins to one where a Ducati became the most desirable sporting motorcycle available. Although its predecessors were very successful machines, it was the 916 that captured the imagination of the motorcycle enthusiast, and even the wider general public. And it wasn't just the style of the 916 that set it apart, either. Functionally, the 916 set a standard for sporting motorcycles that proved difficult to improve upon, even more than a decade later. This was particularly evident on the racetrack, where the 916 virtually ruled the World Superbike Championship between 1994 and 2002.

This book traces the development of the 916, and charts its history on and off the racetrack. It is not a document full of comparative road tests such as can be found in any number of motorcycle journals. The judgements made about various models are my own, but I have used performance data from a variety of authoritative periodicals.

When it comes to technical information, I have relied on the official workshop manuals, in addition to press information. As with all forms of information from companies, often there are discrepancies or contradictions, but I have done my best to ensure the information contained here is as accurate as possible.

As always with projects of this type, it would have been impossible to obtain all the required information and photographic material without the generous assistance of enthusiasts through out the world. Many at Ducati were particularly forthcoming at the time I researched the first edition of this book, but, apart from Livio Lodi, all have since left the company. This book was first published in 2001, and has been updated to include the final versions of the 916 and its derivatives through until 2007.

These projects are always more time-consuming than they appear, and I wouldn't be able to complete them without the support of my wife, Miriam, and two sons, Benjamin and Timothy. Finally, while I have endeavoured to be as accurate as possible, I apologise for any errors in this text.

Ian Falloon

The 851 and 888:
The first liquid-cooled four-valve

Although it could be said that its origins lie as far back as Ing Fabio Taglioni's 98cc Gran Sport, or Marianna, of 1955, the 916 story really starts with the first four-valve twin prepared for the Bol d'Or in 1986. The year 1985 had been an important one in the history of the company. After several decades of production uncertainty under government control, the Varese company of Cagiva finally purchased Ducati that year. It inherited a line-up that consisted of beautiful, but expensive and arguably obsolete bevel-drive V-twins, and the Pantah. All these engines were air-cooled, with two-valve desmodromic cylinder heads, and while the Pantah was an extremely advanced and reliable design, by 1985 its limitations as a racing engine were already apparent. The TT2 had dominated World Formula Two racing from 1980 until 1984, but this was a racing class with little real world prestige. Formula One, Endurance and Superbike was what the new owners, the Castiglioni brothers wanted to compete in and the air-cooled 750 F1 wasn't delivering as expected.

Soon after the Cagiva purchase, the Castiglioni brothers made it known they wanted a more modern engine, not only more suitable for racing, but also one that provided room for future development. They were keen to develop a more modern, four-valve engine and looked to Ing Massimo Bordi to coordinate this project. With an engineering thesis on an

For 1991, the 851 Strada was visually similar to the 1989 and 1990 versions, although there were now upside down Showa forks.

While still based on the Pantah design, the new Desmoquattro engine provided an improved basis for development as a racing engine. So good was this engine that it remained at the top of World Superbike Championship for over ten years.

air-cooled bevel-drive four-valve desmodromic cylinder head completed in 1975, Bordi was an excellent choice. He was also a Formula One car racing enthusiast, and a particular admirer of the Cosworth racing engines. Thus, it was to Cosworth that Bordi turned when it came to the thermodynamic design of the four-valve cylinder head.

In every way, the new engine represented a significant departure for Ducati. Its great designer Fabio Taglioni had been reluctant to embrace four-valve cylinder heads. Both the 1971 Grand Prix 500cc bevel-drive experiment and subsequent belt-drive Armaroli design of 1973 offered no improvement over existing two-valve designs and contributed to

The Desmoquattro engine featured four-valve double overhead camshaft desmodromic cylinder heads. Unlike Bordi's original thesis of 1975, all four rockers were positioned between the camshafts.

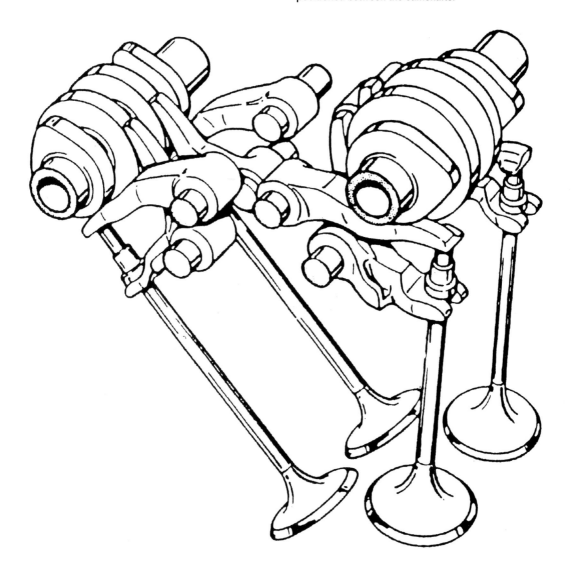

his lack of enthusiasm. Bordi however, was more enthusiastic about modern automobile technology, and it wasn't just the desmodromic four-valve cylinder head that set apart the new design from earlier efforts. With liquid-cooling and electronic fuel-injection, the new engine successfully integrated the best that current technology could provide.

With assistance from Cosworth, a cylinder head was designed with a 40° included valve angle, a centrally located sparkplug, liquid-cooling, and a straight inlet manifold. Cosworth also helped design a suitable exhaust and injection system, but wanted nothing to do with desmodromics. Because the Castiglionis saw this is as an essential ingredient, Bordi

As with all Ducati designs, the 851 was an evolution of an earlier design. Thus the tubular steel frame, and box-section aluminium swingarm with linkage rear suspension, was not unlike that of the final 750 F1 factory racers. No concession was made to engine aesthetics on this early production prototype of 1987.

modified and adapted his earlier design for the new cylinder heads. Instead of the four rockers being located outside the camshafts, all the rockers were now positioned between the camshafts. This early design was called the OVD (Otto Valvole Desmo – eight valve desmo) and would survive until the release of the second generation Testastressa in 2000. The fuel-injection system was the Weber 'IAW Alfa/N' open-loop system, originally developed for the Ferrari F40 sports car, and it suited a twin-cylinder motorcycle perfectly. The electronic control unit was an IAW 043 (07), and this would feature on all 851s (and 888s) through until 1993.

Using modified Pantah crankcases, but with more widely spaced cylinder studs, the prototype engine shared its dimensions with the 750 F1 at 88 x 61.5mm, giving 748cc, and enabling it to be run in the World Endurance Championship. This engine was placed in a modified 750 F1 frame, and the machine

entered in the Bol d'Or 24 Hour endurance race at Paul Ricard on September 18, 1986. Ridden by Marco Lucchinelli, Juan Garriga, and Virginio Ferrari, after 15 hours the new 748 was in seventh place, before retiring with a broken conrod bolt.

These problems almost saw an end to the four-valve project. Taglioni wanted to concentrate on development of the two-valve Pantah engine, and, soon, an 851cc version was producing around 90bhp. It was only when the four-valve engine was increased to a similar 851cc, and there was an immediate 115bhp on the test bench, that the future of the new engine was assured. According to Massimo Bordi, "This was the turning point. I believe that the needle on the test bench of the Ducati company had never ripped past the threshold of 100bhp before."

By early 1987, the engine was now 851cc (92 x 64mm) and reliability improved to the point where it was decided to race it in the

Only a handful of these red and yellow 851 Superbikes
were produced in 1987, but they set the stage for the
run of Tricolore production machines the following year.
These few machines featured 16in Marvic wheels, a
braced swingarm, and a racing exhaust system.

Daytona Battle of the Twins race in March.
Producing a claimed 120bhp at 11,500rpm
at the rear wheel, Marco Lucchinelli easily
won the race. Even more significantly, he was
timed at 165.44mph (266km/h), an incredible
speed for a twin in 1987. Engine reliability was
improved through the use of stronger titanium
Pankl conrods, and larger (42mm, up from
40mm) big-end bearings. Specifically designed
stronger and larger crankcases also allowed for
a six-speed gearbox.

The chassis was a tubular steel space
frame, with a braced aluminium swingarm,
and a linkage rising rate rear suspension
similar to the final racing 750 TT1. As with the
Pantah, the swingarm pivoted on the rear of
the crankcases, and, while the engine was
technologically advanced, the use of the steel
frame retained a link with tradition. There was

however, much room for development with this
early 851. The quest for increased performance
saw reliability suffer, and the piecemeal
development saw the 1987 factory 851 as one
of the ugliest machines ever to emanate from
the Ducati factory at Borgo Panigale. A maze
of pipes and fabrications obliterated the engine,
and the bodywork lacked coherency. However,
by November 1987, the design was considered
complete enough to produce a run of seven
851 Superbikes as a precursor to a general
production run in 1988.

After disappointment in the Italian Superbike
Championship of 1987, more was expected
for 1988. This year was to be the first for the
World Superbike Championship, and, with
the requirement for 200 machines to be built
for homologation, Ducati produced the 851
Superbike Kit and Strada. Known as the

continued on page 15

Early days in World Superbike

The stage was set at Donington on April 3, 1988. Here, former World 500cc Champion Marco Lucchinelli rode the 851 to overall victory in the first ever World Superbike event. It was to be an omen, as the four-valve Ducati was soon to become the dominant machine in this series. Although plagued with engine and electrical problems, Lucchinelli finished fifth overall in that inaugural season. For 1989, Raymond Roche became the official works rider on the 851 (now displacing 888cc), and, with five victories, ended third in the Championship. The 148kg 888 produced 132bhp at 11,500rpm. By 1990, the factory 888 Corsa was much more reliable (though the crankcase problems persisted), and with around 136bhp and only 140kg, Roche went on to win the World Superbike Championship. He won eight races, and team-mate Giancarlo Falappa one.

American Doug Polen took the Championship in 1991. On a Fast by Ferracci 888, Polen completely dominated the season, winning 17 of 26 races. The 888 Corsa weighed close to the class minimum at 143kg, and produced 134bhp at 12,000rpm. Proving this was no 'flash-in-the-pan,' Polen repeated this in 1992, this time on an official factory 888, Roche being relegated to a satellite team. Roche and Falappa came second and fourth in the Championship, the 888s winning 20 races during the season. Although the 888 Sport Production for 1992 featured new styling and revised frames, the factory Corsas still used 1991 frames and bodywork. Consistent development of the 888 saw the power increase to nearly 140bhp.

After some encouraging rides during 1992 on a privateer 888, British rider Carl Fogarty replaced Polen for 1993. With 19 wins spread between Fogarty, Falappa, and privateer Andreas Meklau, Ducati still won the constructor's Championship, although the rider's title went to Kawasaki's Scott Russell. For this final year of the 851-based racer, the engine was enlarged to 926cc. Although power was increased to around 145bhp, this 96 x 64mm engine never performed as well as the later 66mm stroke versions. The Corsas now had bodywork styled along the lines of the SP5, and featured the newer frames without the individually welded top tubes. Despite suspension development that included 45mm Öhlins forks, it was now obvious that the days of the 851-based racers as unbeatable World Championship racers were over.

After a promising start during 1988, Marco Lucchinelli assumed the role as team manager for 1989. Raymond Roche rode the factory 888, now with Öhlins front forks and sometimes shrouded carbon front disc brakes.

A more consistent season in 1990 saw Raymond Roche give Ducati its first World Superbike Championship.

One of the greatest of all Ducati riders was Doug Polen. Here he is on the Fast by Ferracci 888 in 1991. He went on to win back-to-back World Superbike Championships.

Although a machine with a confused identity, the 851 Superbike Kit of 1988 had a certain appeal. This machine was prepared by Bob Brown in Australia for the late Robert Holden.

'Tricolore' because of the distinctive red, white, and green colour scheme, 207 Superbike Kits and 304 Stradas were constructed and sold at a premium price. Unfortunately, while they promised much, they were underdeveloped. The strange equipment typified the idiosyncratic Ducati foibles of that era.

As a homologation special, the 851 Superbike Kit was possibly the more flawed of the two 1988 production versions. Although much of the specification was of a high standard, with a claimed 120bhp, the engine performance was lacking for racing. While the Superbike Kit came shod with racing slicks on 17in magnesium Marvic wheels, and was definitely not street legal, somewhat surprisingly, it also had a headlight, taillight, and electric start. Thus it was decidedly overweight, despite an optimistic claim of 165kg. The dry weight was more in the region of 189kg; this rising to around 200kg fully wet. Although obviously too heavy for a real racing machine, the Superbike Kit did at least offer acceptable handling. This couldn't be said of the more street-orientated 851 Strada that came with Marvic/Akront 16in wheels, and provided unusual steering. These wheels seem to have been left over from the limited edition 750 Montjuich and Santamonica production run, and were unsuited to the larger 851.

The 851 Superbike Kit and Strada may have been limited edition models with many individually fabricated pieces, but they were a disappointment. The Superbike Kit was neither racer nor roadster, and, while the Strada provided exceptional performance for a twin, the premium price ensured many remained unsold through until 1989. Still, the 851 Strada undoubtedly raised the stakes for street motorcycle two-cylinder performance. The Italian magazine *Moto Sprint* has often received the first test machines out of the factory, and it achieved a top speed of

The 888 Corsa (Racing)

Customer racers have long been a feature of Ducati's marketing strategy and, during 1988, in addition to the two production versions of the 851, there was also a full racing specification 888cc Lucchinelli Replica. Still titled the 851 Corsa (Racing), the reality was these Lucchinelli Replicas were a long way removed from the genuine factory bike as raced in the World Superbike Championship. In those early days, there was little information available on the fully mapped Weber injection system and, without specialised knowledge, privateers were at a severe disadvantage. Alternative EPROMs for the 07 control unit weren't readily available and this made tuning difficult.

The 851 Corsa was again offered for 1989, and it continued to be produced over the next few years, the general specification being one year behind that of the official factory machines. Thus, for 1990, the Corsa, now a Roche Replica, featured Öhlins front forks and numerous engine developments that had been successful during 1989. Following the success of the factory bike during 1990, the 851 Racing for 1991 included many more carbon-fibre body parts to reduce the weight to 155kg. However, with a claimed 128bhp at 11,000rpm, it was still a long way removed from the official factory machines.

The 1993 888 Racing was similar in specification to the 1992 factory machines, although it featured the updated frame and bodywork. While the 1993 factory bikes displaced 926cc, these were still 888cc.

Although the production 851 and 888 featured new frames and bodywork, the 1992 888 Racing was more closely related to the 1991 bikes. Thus it retained the earlier frame with separately welded outer sections, as well as the previous tank and seat styling. Further weight reduction, though, saw the 888 Racing weigh only 150kg, and, although power was unchanged, these were now more competitive racers. The 888 Racing for 1993 shared the revised frame and bodywork with the factory bikes, and through the use of more carbon-fibre (such as the footrest brackets), the weight was down to 145kg. While still 888cc (the factory bikes were 926cc that year), larger valve sizes of 36mm and 31mm, and a new exhaust camshaft raised the power to 135bhp at 11,500rpm, at the rear wheel.

Although the factory raced the new 916 during 1994, the customer 888 Racing was essentially the 1993 926cc factory racer. Also 926cc, there was a larger (37mm) inlet valve, 96mm Omega pistons and a claimed 142bhp at 11,500rpm. In line with other 1994 models, the CPU was now an IAW 435 (P8). The frame was altered, too, with the steering head angle now 22½°. Other changes included a new airbox and bigger bored exhaust, 42mm Öhlins suspension and steering damper, a new crankcase breather and tank, and five spoke Marchesini wheels with rim sizes of 3.50 x 17in, and 6.00 x 17in.

851/888 Racing Production Numbers		
Model	Year	Total
851 Racing	1990	20
851 Racing	1991	50
888 Racing	1992	35
888 Racing	1993	46
888 Racing	1994	32

238.7km/h with a standing start 400m in 11.03 seconds at 197.207km/h. While the 1988 851 Strada was flawed, fortunately Ducati made amends with the improved 851 Strada of 1989. Although no longer a limited production model (751 were constructed), functionally the 1989 851 was a vastly improved machine over the Tricolore Strada.

Central to the improvement for 1989 were 17in wheels front and rear, the rim sizes of 3.50in and 5.50in being identical to those on the 851 Superbike Kit. These sizes were state-of-the-art for the time and remain so, identical sizes continuing on the current 996. Also contributing to the superior steering was a reduction in the steering head angle, to 24½°, and less trail at 94mm. Although the Weber IAW 043 (07) injection system now featured only a single injector per cylinder, the engine still had the Pankl H-section conrods. With an 11.0:1 compression ratio, there was a slight power increase to 105bhp at 9000rpm (at the crankshaft). Other improvements over the earlier Tricolore included twin 320mm front discs, though these were no longer the fully floating cast iron type. Setting off the revised 851 Strada was distinctive red paintwork. The 1989 Strada performed similarly to the earlier model, with *Moto Sprint* managing a top speed of 240.9km/h and a standing start 400m time of 11.11 seconds at 194.877km/h.

There were few changes to the 851 Strada for 1990. The Pankl H-section steel conrods were replaced by regular forged conrods, although the engine specifications were otherwise unchanged. The provision of a dual seat saw the dry weight increase to 192kg. Suspension development for 1991 included upside down Showa GD 011 forks and an Öhlins DU 0060 shock absorber, although there was now no longer provision for ride height adjustment. There was a slight reduction in the compression ratio to 10.5:1, and power was 91bhp at 9000rpm at the rear wheel. Still, this wasn't reflected in the performance, and this year saw *Moto Sprint* achieve an almost identical top speed of 239.1km/h. The standing start 400m time was 11.17 seconds at 193.509km/h. As was customary with Ducati development, as the specification altered,

the weight also increased, and the 1991 851 Superbike Strada now weighed in at 199kg.

The final 851 appeared for the 1992 model year, this (and the subsequent 888) basically being a stopgap model until the release of the 916. Although the 916 was essentially ready for production, it was delayed, pending the release of Honda's RC45. Thus the 851 was restyled for 1992, incorporating a steel (rather than aluminium) flip-up fuel tank along the lines of the successful 1990 900 Supersport. There was a new seat section, and a Showa shock absorber replaced the Öhlins. To save on production costs, the frame featured bent outer tubes rather than individually welded sections. The engine now shared the cylinder heads (and 33 and 29mm valves) with the 888 SP4, and power was up to 95bhp at 9000rpm. As always, though, the increase in power came with more weight, now 202kg.

A further delay in the release of the 916 prompted Ducati to release the 888 Strada and 888 SPO (Sport Production Omologato) for 1993. The SPO was a US market only model and thus absent from official publicity material, and consequently is omitted from many publications describing these motorcycles. Yet, while it is a hybrid, it is equally important. The 888 Strada was very much a development of the 1992 851 Strada. Now with the 94 x 64mm 888cc engine, all the other specifications were shared with the 1992 851. Power was up to 100bhp at 9000rpm; this engine also powering the SPO. After serial number 000508, the electronic fuel-injection system now incorporated an updated IAW 435 (P8) central processing unit instead of the 043 (07). As expected, the 888 Strada provided slightly improved performance over the 851, and was generally a more civilised machine. *Moto Sprint* achieved a top speed of 245.9km/h, with a standing start 400m time of 10.96 seconds at 203.840km/h. The cooking 888 certainly offered respectable performance for 1993.

Because the SP5 couldn't pass US registration requirements, the SPO was sold to homologate the 888 Racing for AMA Superbike, but it was a much softer machine than the SP5. The engine had single injectors, and there was no external oil cooler. Apart from

continued on page 21

The Sport Production 851 and 888

For 1989, the first development of the 851 Strada was produced for Italian Sport Production, and was initially known only as the 851 Sport Production. The Italian Sport Production series pitted production 750cc fours against twins of up to 1000cc. These early versions were virtually indistinguishable from the Strada, and reputedly 110 were produced. However, this isn't evident in Ducati's official production figures, because they were included with the regular 851 Strada production. The engines were not 888cc as had been documented in other publications, but still had dimensions of 92 x 64mm, giving 851cc. 83mm pistons were also available, providing 869.4cc, a one millimetre overbore being allowed under the Italian regulations. The camshafts were from the earlier 851 Superbike Kit, but, as with the 851 Strada of 1989, there was only a single injector per cylinder. As with all Sport Productions, there was also an external oil cooler. With the top of the airbox removed, power was 122bhp at 10,000rpm, at the crankshaft. The chassis was pure Strada, including the 320mm stainless steel front discs, and the weight was 180kg.

A more impressive Sport Production was offered for 1990: the 851 SP2. This was one of the finest Ducatis of the modern era and differed from the regular 851 Strada in a number of details. In every respect, it was a considerably higher specification machine, particularly in the engine. Although still titled an 851, the engine displaced 888cc through larger (94mm) pistons. There was a return to twin injectors per cylinder (still with the 07 control unit), and, while the 1990 851 Strada featured

regular forged conrods, the 851 SP retained the H-section Pankl rods. The SP2 also featured an entirely different gearbox to that of the regular 851 (and earlier SP), with revised ratios for 3rd, 4th, 5th, and 6th gears, and a closer overall pattern. Power was 109bhp at the rear wheel, and the chassis upgraded to include upside down Öhlins FG 9050 front forks, an Öhlins shock absorber, and fully floating 320mm Brembo cast iron front disc brakes. Completing the improvement was an aluminium rear subframe, but the weight climbed to 188kg because of the heavier forks. Although more 851 SP2s were produced than the first SP, it was still a limited production machine and provided performance hitherto unknown for a twin-cylinder motorcycle. *Moto Sprint* managed to obtain an impressive 258.1km/h out of its test SP2, with a standing start 400m time of 10.85 seconds at 204.571km/h. This was even faster than comparable 750cc fours in 1990.

There was a similar 851 SP3 for 1991 (also 888cc), the most identifiable difference being the more upswept exhaust pipes. These were homologation exhausts for the factory racers and resulted in a small power increase to 111bhp at 10,500rpm. Improvement generated through racing saw stronger crankcases and clutch, and, like the SP2, the SP3 was a fantastic high-performance machine. As tested by *Moto Sprint,* the SP3 had a top speed of 261.1km/h, and went through the standing start 400m in 10.78 seconds at 207.664km/h. A small number of 851 Sport Production Specials were also produced for 1991 (16), these having an even higher performance engine and more carbon-fibre. However, the factory did not

Some of the most impressive of all production Ducatis were the 888cc Sport Production series. Here an SP4 of 1992 is flanked by a 1991 SP3 (left) and 1993 SP5 (right).

Although the SP5 no longer featured Öhlins front forks, the engine specification was even higher than that of the SP2, 3, and 4. The 916 may overshadow them, but the 888 Sport Production series were fantastic motorcycles.

officially list the 851 SPS, and it seems that they were available only to those with good connections at the factory. For 1992, however, there were two officially listed 888 Sport Production models: the SP4 and SPS.

Now with '888' decals and a large '1' on the fairing, the SP4 and SPS also shared the new styling of the 1992 851 Superbike Strada. This included a revised fuel tank and seat, although the Sport Production still featured a solo seat. While the SP4 engine was the same as that of the SP3, the 888 SPS (Sport Production Special) was one of the strongest ever performing production Ducatis. The engine specification of the SPS was similar to that of the Corsa, with larger valves (34 and 30mm) and hotter camshafts giving 120bhp at 10,500rpm. The cooling system (without a radiator fan) also came from the Corsa, and a carbon-fibre fuel tank saw the weight reduced to 185kg. Offering such an incredible power-to-weight ratio, along with top quality suspension components, the 888

SPS was undoubtedly one of the finest Ducatis of the pre-916 era. Even by today's standards, performance of the 888 SPS was impressive. *Moto Sprint* put one through the timing lights at 268km/h, with a standing 400m time of 10.39 seconds at 212.015km/h.

The final 888 Sport Production was the 888 SP5 of 1993. With the higher performance SPS engine (but with an SP4 cooling system and 118bhp at 10,500rpm), the SP5 featured less expensive suspension components and a normal steel fuel tank. There was a newer IAW 435 (P8) CPU, the engine still featuring twin injectors. Showa GD 061 forks replaced the expensive Öhlins forks that had graced all the Sport Production series since the SP2, although an Öhlins DU8071 unit was retained on the rear. There were the new colours and graphics for all 1993 model year Ducatis, and the SP5 featured carbon-fibre mufflers and a fully-floating rear disc brake. The '1' now appeared on the seat rather than the fairing. The performance, too, didn't quite match that of the 1992 888 SPS, but it was still pretty impressive. As tested by *Moto Sprint*, the SP5 managed a top speed of 260.3km/h, with a standing start 400m time of 10.57 seconds at 210.226km/h.

The 888 Sport Production series may now be overshadowed by the 916/996, but in many ways they represent the end of an era for Ducati. There was a rawness about these machines that appealed in the way of earlier Ducatis. They were still Ducatis for the traditionalist, and they were also built in far fewer numbers than later versions.

851/888 SP Production Numbers		
Model	Year	Total
851 SP2	1990	380
851 SP3	1991	534
851 SPS	1991	16
888 SP4	1992	500
888 SPS	1992	101
888 SP5	1993	500

As the Sport Production series had displaced 888cc since 1990, it was inevitable that the 851 Strada would also eventually become an 888. This occurred in 1993 with the underrated 888 Strada.

lower spec Showa GD 011 forks, the chassis was straight off the SP5. The SPO had the single seat, upswept exhaust pipes (without carbon-fibre mufflers), and Öhlins shock absorber (along with eccentric ride height adjustment), of the SP5. It was, however, built in even fewer numbers than the SP5, with 290 built for 1993, plus a further 100 for the 1994 model year towards the end of 1993. The 1993 versions featured black wheels, and for 1994 the wheels were gold. The 1994 series SPO also included a numbered plaque on the top triple clamp.

Rather than being designed from the outset as a balanced structure between the engine, frame and suspension, the 851/888 evolved from continuous development. Thus the frame owed its origins to that of the 1985 750 TT1 factory racer, and the suspension and wheels were altered gradually to allow for the development of racing tyres. By 1993, the 888 was a nicely homogenised machine, but exhibited deficiencies as a racer. The engine support structure, with the engine being located by only two bolts to the frame, was a relic of the days of the TT2, a tiny 122kg machine that produced 76bhp. With the swingarm pivoting on the crankcases, as with all Pantahs, the frame was placed under considerable stress, especially the rigidity between the swingarm and the steering head. As the racing 888s became more powerful, the deficiencies of the

structure of the frame became more evident.

There was also the problem of the length and weight distribution. The 1430mm wheelbase of the 888 was simply too long, and the engine placed too far back in the chassis, for a high powered Superbike racer. On top of that, the 888, although not too heavy, was wide. There was really no concerted effort to style the machine, as Ducati had never had an official design department. Some earlier designs had been entrusted to outside contractors, but, in the case of the 851/888m the styling was an evolution from the first, rather ugly, 748. This piecemeal approach to development also led to a machine that was difficult to work on. Anyone who has had to perform a valve adjustment on an early 851 can testify to that. The design of the next generation four-valve Ducati was assigned to Massimo Tamburini, who took a completely different approach. Although using essentially the same ingredients, and also continuing Ducati's philosophy of evolution, with the 916 Tamburini achieved an amazing transformation. In the process, he gave Ducati possibly its greatest design ever, and the first Ducati that was no longer only a machine for the enthusiast or cognoscenti. With the 916, Tamburini created a mainstream motorcycle with universal appeal, and, in the process, provided the company with a new lease of life.

The development of the 916

As the piecemeal approach to the development of the 888 continued, year after year, at Bologna, unbeknown to most outsiders, work on an evolutionary four-valve Ducati was steadily proceeding. During 1984, Massimo Tamburini became the head of the new COR Cagiva design studio. Rather than Varese, where Cagiva was based, this was situated at Tamburini's hometown of Rimini, because Tamburini wanted to be closer to his parents, who, at the time, were unwell. Tamburini's first complete design for Cagiva was the Ducati Paso of 1985, and, with its all-enveloping bodywork, this represented a controversial and all-new approach for a Ducati. The Paso may not have been universally accepted, but it showed that Tamburini was prepared to chart new paths; this fitted with the Castiglionis' vision for Ducati's future.

Although the 851 was being developed at Bologna during 1987, the Castiglionis realised there was a need to develop the new four-valve Ducati as a total engineering package, with fully coordinated styling. Thus, even as Bordi and his team were developing the 851, Tamburini was given the charter to create the 916, although, at that time, the 916cc version of the engine was still some way in the future. As the design centre expanded, it became Il Centro Ricerche Cagiva (CRC), and moved to the nearby hilltop Republic of San Marino.

Although the 888 was proving a winner in the World Superbike series, in reality much of this success was due to a significant weight advantage and higher-class riders, rather than superior engineering. In addition to the 1000cc capacity limit for twins, compared to 750cc for fours, the twins also had a 25kg weight benefit. While it had taken a few years for Ducati to get the weight of its 888 Corsa close to the class minimum of 140kg, by 1991 it was very close, making the 888 virtually unbeatable. With the dominance of Polen during that 1991 season, it was obvious that this weight advantage wouldn't last forever and the days of the 888cc racer were limited. However, the regulations were slow to change, possibly because Italians ran the World Superbike Championship, and it wasn't until 1993 that the weight limit for twins was increased to 145kg. The failure of Carl Fogarty to secure the rider's title in 1993 gave Ducati further respite, so that for 1994 the fours received only a 5kg reduction in minimum weight, to 160kg.

This really played into Ducati's hands; by 1994, Ducati was well prepared for these changes to the regulations. Ducati's long-term plan called for a gradual increase in the displacement of the four-valve engine to close to the 1000cc limit, eventually accompanied by a new design that would see it competitive beyond the turn of the century. This wasn't to be just a new chassis, but a complete evolution, including significant engine

One of the final design sketches of 1991. Even at this late stage the capacity is still 888cc.

development. Unlike the 851 and 888 that had grown out of the 750 TT1, the chassis would be designed to accommodate a full litre engine, and to comfortably handle the expected power increase. And, like all great Ducati designs preceding it, it was intended for the racetrack first, with street versions to follow.

With the assistance of Massimo Parenti, and an initial team comprising just four engineers, Tamburini embarked on the 916 project during 1988. This spanned almost six years because of interruptions to work on other motorcycle designs, including Randy Mamola's Cagiva C588 and C589 500 Grand Prix machines of 1988 and 1989, the 1987 Cagiva 125 Freccia, and the Mito two years later. Codenamed the 2887 project, work on the geometrical aspect of the 916 frame took place over a two-year period, even before the construction of a prototype. By the time the

project moved to San Marino, the workforce comprised 25 young specialists, all motorcycle enthusiasts. Tamburini eventually eschewed the Japanese- and Bimota-style aluminium deltabox frame in preference for the traditional Ducati spaceframe. All along, development was done in consultation with Massimo Bordi at Bologna, and, while there had been serious consideration given to an aluminium frame similar to that on the TGA1 Grand Prix racer, tradition won, and the 916 retained its links with earlier Ducatis. Ducati's custom had always been one of evolution, and Massimo Bordi wanted the 916 to be an evolution of the 851 concept. Tubular steel frames were a medium that Tamburini was very familiar with, too, not only from his earlier Bimota motorcycles, but also from thermo-hydraulic systems. From Ducati's racing experience with the 851 and 888, the requirements for the 916 included a

Massimo Tamburini

When he came to Cagiva, Massimo Tamburini was already well known to the motorcycle fraternity. Born in Rimini on 28 November 1943, Tamburini was one of the founders of Bimota (along with Valerio Bianchi and Giuseppe Morri), in 1966. In 1983, he left the small Rimini concern, after a disagreement with Giuseppe Morri over the company's future direction. Bimota was originally a company specialising in heating and air-conditioning systems, but Tamburini was a long-time motorcycle enthusiast and his first frame design was for an MV Agusta 600. His father had ridden Moto Guzzis, and Tamburini's heroes were Renzo Pasolini (after whom he named the Ducati Paso), and the great Guzzi engineer Giulio Carcano. Tamburini's later success in creating an alternative frame for the CB750 Honda saw the establishment of Bimota Meccanica in 1973. Bimota then went on to become one of the most successful and innovative

independent frame manufacturers, producing a series of spectacular aftermarket frames, initially for a range of Japanese engines, but, later, also Ducati. Along the way, Tamburini introduced engineering features that would later become commonplace, including rising-rate suspension, curved swingarms, and perimeter frames. Soon after leaving Bimota, he became involved with the Roberta Gallina TGA1 500cc Grand Prix racer, but, as this was perceived as being too radical for Suzuki, the project folded at the end of 1985. As the Gallina team was owned by Cagiva, Tamburini was concurrently involved with projects for Ducati, these including a revised Mille and tubular-framed 750, both not venturing past the prototype stage. More recently he has earned considerable acclaim for the design of the spectacular 750cc four-cylinder MV F4 and has earned a reputation as one of the world's leading, and most innovative, motorcycle designers.

Members of the CRC 916 design team with their creation at the official release in 1994. At the back on the left is Massimo Parenti, with Massimo Tamburini in the centre.

Although the Desmoquattro engine was almost identical to that of the 888, the entire motorcycle was more compact, with every component designed to occupy as little space as possible.

reduction in the wheelbase from the 888, whilst providing as close to 50/50 weight distribution as attainable, along with adequate wheel travel. Considering the length of the Ducati engine, this meant placing the front wheel as close to the engine as possible. Thus the engine was rotated forward 1.5° to help the front tyre clear the cylinder head.

With the importance of the 916 spearheading Ducati's racing future, the frame and suspension testing was done by Davide Tardozzi at the nearby racetrack of Mugello. With an 888 as a bench mark, when the definitive frame configuration was completed in January 1992 the result gave a wheelbase of 1410mm (compared to 1430mm for the 888), with 49% of weight on the front wheel. Built by Cagiva Telaio, the diameter of the main tubing (25 CrMo4) was 28mm (compared to 25mm on the 888), with the secondary tubing being the same as that on the 888 at 22mm. In the interests of mass production, the frame was MIG-welded. An important element of the frame design was an additional lower engine support, also contributing to increased rigidity, with the swingarm being supported by the frame in addition to the engine cases, as on the 888. Measurements by Tamburini and Parenti of the bare 916 frame registered a figure of 2745 Nm/° of deflection, the comparable figure for the 851/888 being 2140 Nm/°. An important component of the structure was the sealed airbox, situated between the top frame tubes, with the lower part of the 17-litre fuel tank forming the top of the airbox. With a plastic airbox installed, the torsional rigidity increased to 2824 Nm/°. However, with a carbon-fibre airbox, this increased 20% to 3269 Nm/° of deflection. Unfortunately, the benefits of the carbon-fibre airbox were reserved for the racing and some Sport Production versions. The inconsistency in the specification of the early Sport Production series saw some receive

The airbox was an important contributor to frame rigidity, and was sealed by the lower part of the fuel tank. Mounting the steering damper transversely was also innovative.

the carbon-fibre airbox and some the plastic version. The plastic airboxes were also of poor quality and very prone to breakage. Because the early 916 was conceived as a monoposto, the rear subframe was aluminium, like the solo seat 888 Sport Production.

Tamburini was also intent on creating an extremely strong steering head structure, the tubing being 80mm in outer diameter, with special bearings to allow for a thick (35mm) steering tube. An important element in the design was the incorporation of adjustable caster without altering the wheelbase. Press releases at the time stated 24-25° with 94-100mm of trail, but, according to the official workshop manual, the standard setting was 24°30', giving 97mm of trail, this being

steepened to 23°30' with 91mm of trail for racing. The alteration in caster was achieved by ellipsoidal bearings in the steering tube, but, with the steeper setting, the steering lock no longer worked.

Another important consideration in the design was a reduction in frontal area and an improvement in aerodynamics over the 851/888. This led to the small overall size of the motorcycle, and the shape of the fairing, fuel tank, and seat. From above, the shape was intentionally designed to emulate the curves of a woman. Part of the Tamburini philosophy was to feature individually designed components for every part of the motorcycle, thus little of the chassis was shared with the earlier 888. Although the first prototype I saw in September 1993 featured an Öhlins front fork and rear shock absorber, all the production 916s had Showa forks. These 43mm GD 051 front forks were specially constructed by Showa and provided 127mm of wheel travel. There were also ten possible adjustments for rebound damping, twelve adjustments for compression damping, and a 15mm range for spring preload. An important feature of the front end was the design of the triple clamps, these being machined in pairs, the lower triple clamp being notable for its exceptional depth. This unique and exquisitely chill-cast lower triple clamp was an important feature, and indicative of the attention to detail that Tamburini and his team paid to significant components. It also provided increased rigidity, and undoubtedly contributed to the magnificent handling by the 916.

With a stated intention of returning to endurance racing, the swingarm was single-sided to allow for rapid wheel changes. In the early 1990s, Ducati still dreamed of winning both the Suzuka Eight-hour race and the Bol d'Or, and the 916 was designed with this goal in mind. A special endurance 888 had been prepared during 1991, but had proved

These 1992 drawings indicate the eventual shape of the fairing and headlights. This was such a successful design that, even nearly a decade on, the style still looks good, and has stood the test of time.

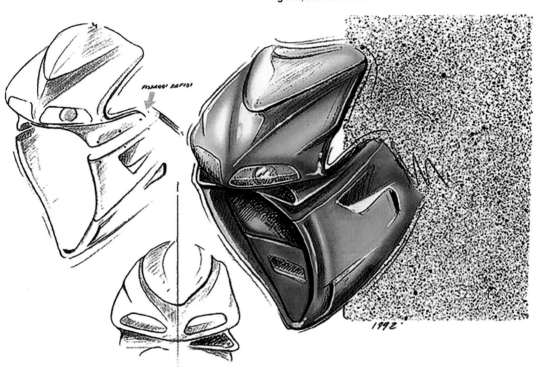

unreliable. Although a successful return to endurance racing has also eluded the 916, the design has lived with the single-sided swingarm throughout its life. Much of the swingarm design was done by computer, at the Cagiva Racing department at Varese, by the Cagiva engineer Albesiano. An important part of the design was the inclusion of bearings in the swingarm for additional support. These were twin roller bearings on the drive side, and twin ball bearings on the right.

The associated pushrod linkage was entrusted to Claudio Domenicali at Bologna. Although difficult to set up for racing, this linkage, with teflon-lined spherical bearings, has proven extremely successful. With Honda holding the ELF patent for single-sided swingarms, it was important for the Ducati design to circumvent this patent. Constructed of chill-cast aluminium, the swingarm of the

first production 916 was stronger than that of the comparable Honda, and, at 475mm long, 19mm shorter than that of the 888. Later, however, it would become necessary to lengthen the swingarm slightly for racing, to improve traction and weight distribution. An important feature was the incorporation of a large eccentric hub for chain adjustment, the hollow axle being 35mm in diameter. The rear suspension was by a Showa GD052-007-02, with a stroke of 71mm providing 130mm of wheel travel. This was also possibly the weakest standard chassis component.

A steering damper was included as integral to the design: this being positioned behind the top triple clamp, and mounted transversely. It was another example of Tamburini's unique and pure approach to motorcycle design. The non-adjustable Sachs-Boge steering damper provided a neutral response to steering input

Tamburini's attention to detail was evident in the
specifically manufactured three-spoke 17in Brembo
'Ducati Racing' wheels. The axle diameter was 35mm.

The integration of the seat, twin taillights and mufflers on the 916 was inspired.

because of its symmetrical action. Continuing the path of deviation from the 888 were specifically manufactured three-spoke 17in Brembo wheels, although still retaining the same 3.50in and 5.50in rim widths. These wheels featured hollow elliptical spokes with variable cross-sections. The tyres specified were either Pirelli Dragon, or Michelin (MTR 01 /02 or TX 11/23). Although the standard rear tyre size was a 190/50 ZR17, a 180/55 ZR17 could also be fitted. The final

drive was by a DID 525 HV ($\frac{5}{16}$ x $\frac{5}{8}$in) chain, up in dimensions from the 520 chain fitted to the 888.

When it came to the brakes, little was different to those of the 888. At the front were the same warp-prone stainless steel 320 x 5mm discs that featured on all other regular production Ducatis. With Brembo P4 30/34 'Gold Series' brake calipers and a PS 16mm master cylinder with a remote reservoir, these didn't provide exceptional

continued on page 34

The Supermono

Although the Supermono project began after the 916, the Supermono prototype was unveiled a year earlier, at the Cologne Show at the end of 1992. It caused a sensation, and has remained one of the most beautiful and timeless of all Ducati designs. Intended for 'Sound of Singles' racing, the Supermono was a catalogue racer, much the same as the 888 Racing, and produced by the racing department. The heart of the Supermono was the engine, a design based on that of the 888 but featuring a number of significant developments. To achieve the perfect primary balance of a 90° V-twin, Massimo Bordi essentially created a single out of the twin. However, in place of the second piston he placed a pivoting lever attached to the second Pankl titanium conrod. Called the doppia bielletta, or double conrod, this effectively made the large single as smooth as a twin. It was a brilliant conception, as anyone who has ridden a Supermono can testify.

In other respects, the Supermono was closely related to the 888 Racing. Along with liquid-cooling, and the double overhead camshaft four valve desmodromic cylinder head, the same Weber IAW Alfa/N fuel-injection system was used, with twin injectors and a 435 (P8) CPU. The throttle body diameter was 50mm, the valve sizes 37mm and 31mm, and the camshafts the same as the 1994

888 Racing (926cc). There were, however, some departures from the 888 Racing, the most important being the use of 49mm plain main bearings, and the water pump driven off the exhaust camshaft. With dimensions of 100 x 70mm the engine of the first production version displaced 549cc. The piston was a British Omega, weighing 460g and, with an 11.8:1 compression ratio, the claimed power was 75bhp at 10,000rpm. Many engine components were specific to the Supermono, including the crankcases, cylinders, and crankshaft. There were all new gearbox ratios and a dry, 180-watt alternator. Thus the Supermono featured a revised magnesium left side engine cover and the overall engine width reduced over the twin.

Developed by Claudio Domenicali and Luigi Mengoli, when the Supermono was first displayed it had stunning bodywork designed by Pierre Terblanche at Cagiva Morrazone in Varese. As a high specification Corsa, all the chassis components were of the highest quality. This included a tubular steel space-frame in ALS 500, 42mm Öhlins front forks, and an Öhlins DU 2041 rear cantilever suspension. The frame in particular was TIG-welded, and beautifully and individually crafted in a way that no production frame could be. The frame was obviously intended only for limited production, even the 916 frame appearing crude

Although based on the 888, the Supermono engine featured a revised water pump location and dry alternator under the magnesium engine cover. The bump for the dummy conrod can be seen, as can the low engine height.

Undoubtedly one of the most spectacular modern motorcycle designs, all the Supermono bodywork was carbon-fibre. This is a 550cc 1994 version.

by comparison. The front forks were very similar to those used on the 888 Racing and were almost excessive for the tiny Supermono. Completing the racing specification were magnesium Marchesini wheels (MT 3.50 x 17in and MT 5.00 x 17in) and racing specification Brembo brakes. At the front were twin 280mm fully floating cast iron discs with P4.30-34 calipers with a 190mm rear disc and P32A caliper. The 1360mm wheelbase was 20mm less than Bordi originally anticipated. In order to keep the weight down to 122kg, every body part was made of carbon-fibre.

Apart from the ability to rev to previously unheard of levels for a big single, much of the racetrack ability of the Supermono was due to the remarkably low centre of gravity. Continuing the path exhibited by the great Ing Giulio Cesare Carcano with his Moto Guzzi racing horizontal singles of the 1950s, the Supermono provided exceptional handling. This was ably demonstrated by its ability to circulate a racetrack at speeds comparable to those of a 100bhp 600 Supersport. The author's experience

with a Supermono indicated it to be the finest handling motorcycle he had experienced. This flawless handling offered everything; stability, agility, quick steering, and amazing response.

For 1995, developments included a 102mm piston giving 572cc, a new EPROM and silencer, and slightly different suspension. The front forks were now 42mm Öhlins FG 9311, with a DU 2042 rear unit. However, in the world of Sound of Singles racing, the engine was now too small to be as competitive as it was back in 1993 and there were to be no further batches. With the consideration of a production version during 1998, a Supermono engine was installed in a 900 Supersport frame as a prototype, but only one ended up being constructed. Although the Supermono engine had been designed with the possibility of including an electric start, there was no provision made for a sidestand and it would have required re-tooling for series production. There had been talk of a production Supermono: this continuing for many years after its introduction in 1993, but never came to fruition.

	1992	1993	1994	1995	TOTAL
550 Supermono Racing Production Numbers	1	30	10	25	66

braking. The early models also lacked adjustable brake and clutch levers and, with rubber brake lines and Fren-do 222 brake pads, gave a soft brake feel. At the rear was a smaller, 220 x 6mm, steel disc, with a 'Gold Series' P2 105N caliper and PS11mm master cylinder.

Although these brakes weren't anything special compared to the 888, it was the details such as the footpegs and levers, instruments and taillight that set the 916 apart. Every component had been individually designed and crafted for the 916, much in the style of Tamburini's previous work at Bimota. Many parts were unique and not shared with other Ducatis. These included bolts, rubber wire retainers, and banjo fittings with hollowed out heads. Nothing exemplified the attention to detail more than the beautifully executed headlight support and the twin poly-ellipsoidal headlights. These alone created a style unlike any other and, despite attempts by others to emulate it, it remains unique and timeless. Completing the unique style were specifically styled twin taillights, and an exhaust system that was more than purely a set of exhaust pipes and mufflers. Designed to aid aerodynamics more than ultimate power, this system also provided excellent access to the rear wheel. With 45mm header pipes, these went into a muffled collector before exiting to 45mm muffler pipes and 110mm mufflers. Again, with the twin mufflers exiting under the seat, the 916 was groundbreaking in style, and still hasn't been successfully emulated.

Indicative of the overall attention to detail evident in the design was that entire engine assembly was devised to be easily removed as a single unit. This was despite the extremely compact fitting of all the components in the frame. The resulting motorcycle, too, was lighter than the 888 Strada, with a dry weight of 198kg (as opposed to 210kg for the 888).

It wasn't only the chassis that came in for consideration with Tamburini's new design. With a goal to make a full litre engine someway in the future, the 851/888/926 stroke of 64mm was deemed too short. Thus Massimo Bordi and his engineering team at Borgo Panigale lengthened the stroke by 2mm, to 66mm. With 94mm pistons similar to those from the 888 Sport Production, this gave 916cc; hence the designation of the new motorcycle as the 916. These pistons provided an 11:1 compression ratio. On the first 916 Strada, there were steel Pankl H-section conrods, each weighing 500g. Despite the longer stroke, the conrod length stayed the same, at 124mm eye-to-eye, giving a 1.88:1 stroke-to-rod length ratio. This conrod length was inherited from the 500cc Pantah and was used on the 750 F1 (61.5mm stroke) as well as the 851/888. While it may not have been the ideal 2:1 stroke-to-rod length ratio, the resulting 916 provided considerably superior power characteristics to any of the earlier 851 and 888cc engines. It was almost as if the engine had been crying out for the 2mm longer stroke from its inception. Other conrod dimensions, too, were shared with the 888, these being the 45mm big-end journal, and 20mm gudgeon. The general engine design, though, was identical to that of the 888, except that the problematic smaller left side RHP main bearing was improved. This was now of better material and incorporated an additional ball.

The valve sizes on the 916 Strada came from the 888 Strada and SP, at 33mm and 29mm, though the cylinder head was initially designed to accept up to 38mm inlet and 31mm exhaust valves for racing. The camshafts for the 916 Strada were also identical to those of the earlier 888 Strada. All the gear ratios, too, were shared with the 888 Strada, including the 31/62 2:1 primary drive. The clutch for the 916 Strada carried a code of 19020013A, and was also shared with 900 Supersports and the

Without the bodywork, the dense structure of the 916 is clearly evident. A component that the CRC design team was proud of was the specially cast headlight support.

888. It consisted of two 2mm driven plates, one 3mm driving plate, a 1.5mm spring plate, and six driving plates (3mm) alternated with six driven plates (2mm).

The Weber electronic injection and ignition system included a single injector, a 50mm throttle body, and the usual IAW 435 (P8) CPU with an 054 EPROM. The CPU was mounted under the tailpiece, above the twin mufflers. A 350-watt alternator provided the power for the electrical system, and there was

a new regulator. This, however, still didn't overcome the electrical problems that had plagued Ducatis since they were created and the regulator in particular was problematic. To facilitate the fitting of the engine in the new frame, there were slight revisions to the cooling system, along with an increase in the surface area of the curved radiator. Changes to the lubrication system included an external oil cooler similar to that of the 888 Sport Production.

Two generations of classic Ducati. The 750 Super Sport of 1974 has long been hailed as the ultimate production Ducati, but the 916 has undoubtedly been a more significant model in the history of the company.

With the sealed airbox fed by a ram intake with filters in the ducts, the initial claimed power of the 916 Strada was increased slightly over that over the 110bhp 888 Strada, to a modest 114bhp at 9000rpm (at the crankshaft). Later however, this power figure was revised to 109bhp. Yet it wasn't really the power that was the issue with the 916. Despite being able to achieve a top speed of 260km/h, there were faster and more powerful motorcycles available. Although it was technically only an evolution of the 851, such was the brilliance of the execution of the design that it was almost as if the 916 was a completely new model. The 916 offered more than engine performance, and provided a balance between the engine and chassis that set new standards. Unlike

the 888 (and most earlier Ducatis) there was a homogeneity about the design that took the 916 into another dimension.

What the 916 undoubtedly did for Ducati was take the company beyond that of an enthusiast niche market manufacturer to that of the creator of a universally admired and desirable motorcycle, much as Ferrari had done in the automotive field. When it was first displayed at the Milan Show at the end of 1993, the 916 caused a sensation, even more so than the Supermono had at Cologne the previous year. Visually it was revolutionary and was one of the most beautifully balanced and aesthetically satisfying street motorcycles ever conceived. Unlike most production Ducatis of the 1980s, there was no weakness in the styling. From the

The seat and rear section was a pioneering style and beautifully executed.

distinctive dual headlights through to the seat, the 916 was without peer. Previous Ducatis had sometimes suffered through having to adapt a racing design for the street, but the 916 successfully circumvented this problem. But it was only after success on the racetrack and in the press that the 916 finally assumed the status of the world's most desirable sporting motorcycle. Since its release in 1994, the 916 has gone on to become undoubtedly the greatest Ducati ever. If it wasn't for the significant numbers produced, and the annual developments and improvements, the 916 would even surpass the legendary 1974 750

Super Sport as the ultimate production Ducati. No other Ducati has had such success on the track for such a long period and remained at the top of the performance world for so long. That first 750 Super Sport and its subsequent developments only represented the pinnacle of overall motorcycle sporting performance for two or three years. The 916 and its descendants have provided the class-leading standard for close to a decade. Considering the level of competition, both from Japanese and European manufacturers, that is an extraordinary achievement and is testimony to the genius of its creator, Massimo Tamburini.

The 916 1994-98

After the excitement of the launch of the 916 at the Milan Show of 1993, it was surprising that the eventual production models were very slow to materialise. This scenario would have been expected of Ducati during the 1970s and early 1980s, but was hardly anticipated under the Cagiva regime. Unfortunately, it was a sign that all was not well with Cagiva financially, and, when a fire engulfed the paint shop at Borgo Panigale, production of the 916 was moved to the Cagiva plant at Varese. Because of this disaster, no production 916s were produced at Bologna during 1994, and, as such, the 1994 models don't appear on the official factory production records.

The production 916 Strada for 1994 closely followed that of the four early examples produced at Bologna at the end of 1993. Because of the long and intensive incubation period, there were remarkably few problems for a new model: on early examples, the steering damper could interfere with the fuel tank and, from July 1994, a modified damper support rectified this. There were also some problems with loosening of the screws retaining the rear sprocket and brake disc (from frame number 000001 to 001507). Continuing problems with oil leaks from the crankcase halves eventually saw the implementation of silicon sealant Omnivisc 1002 instead of a gasket (from frame number 001108), as used on the 916 SP. Somewhat later (in April 1997), all 1994 solo seat 916s (until frame number 003097) were

continued on page 43

The style of the 916 was unique, and in 1994 it represented a significant leap forward. Even the later 996 R looked amazingly similar.

The 916 SP (1994-96)

Because the limited edition 851 and 888 Sport Production series had been so successful, it wasn't surprising to see this formula continued, with the release of the 916 during 1994. Engine developments for the 916 SP over the 1994 916 Strada included significantly lighter (349g) titanium H-section Pankl conrods and twin fuel injectors per cylinder (still with the P8 CPU). The cast alloy throttle bodies were also 50mm, but these were identical to the 888 SP5, and differed from those of the 916 Strada (as did the linkage system). The 916 SP also had a different, 057 EPROM and, as with the earlier SP series, too, the 916 SP also featured twin roller main bearings. Another distinguishing feature was cylinder heads based on those of the 916 Racing without the cast 'DESMO 4V DOHC' lettering. The SP cylinder head casting was shorter above the exhaust camshaft for extra front wheel clearance, particularly under racing conditions. The crankcases on the SP also featured a drilled M8 x 75mm crankcase retaining screw beneath the gearbox, for extra strength. As it was found that the crankcase and alternator cover gaskets

had leaked under racing conditions, all 916 SPs used Omnivisc 1002 adhesive instead of gaskets. Another development of the SP over the Strada was a modified lubrication system that came from the racing 888. This featured forced lubrication to the piston gudgeon pins through a gallery in the conrod, while the Strada utilised splash oil feed.

A feature of all Sport Productions that carried over to the 916 SP was the significant increase in claimed horsepower over the Strada. Thus, as with the earlier SP5, the 916 SP had larger valves (34mm inlet and 30mm exhaust), and more radical camshaft timing. Combined with an 11.2:1 compression ratio, the 916 SP produced 126bhp at 10,500rpm (at the crankshaft). This was later revised to 131bhp, possibly to accentuate the differences between the Strada and SP, because there were no engine developments. Unlike the earlier 888 SP that featured its own close ratio gearbox, the 916 SP shared its gearbox with the 916 Strada. However, the clutch was carried over from the 888 SP4 and SP5. With a code of 19020041A, there was one 2mm driven plate, one

A small number of 916 SPs were also available for 1994, these featuring a white number plate on the solo seat. The 916 SP upheld Sport Production tradition, but didn't offer as significant performance boost over the 916 Strada as the earlier 888 SP had over the 851 and 888 Strada.

1.5mm spring plate, one 2.5mm driving plate, one 1.5mm driven plate, six driving plates (2.5mm) alternated with five driven plates (2mm), another 1.5mm driven plate, and, lastly, a 2.5mm driving plate. Some 916 SPs also came with a drilled clutch basket, and the 916 SP also had the larger 350-watt alternator of the 916 Strada, rather than the smaller alternator of the earlier 888 SP. As with earlier SPs, there was a larger-diameter exhaust system, too, the collector box being unmuffled and interfacing the 45mm header pipes with a 50mm collector box and mufflers. The SP also came with additional Termignoni carbon-fibre mufflers, with an alternative 50mm racing exhaust system available. As maximum power was produced at higher revs, the SP also received lower final drive gearing, a 14-tooth sprocket replacing the Strada's 15-tooth.

Although the basic chassis was similar to that of the 916 Strada, the SP featured an Öhlins DU 3420 rear shock absorber and a number of carbon-fibre body parts. These included a front mudguard, chainguard, rear brake line guard, licence plate holder, exhaust pipe insulation, front lower fairing panel, under-seat tray, and occasionally panels

A feature of the 916 SP was fully floating cast iron 320mm Brembo front disc brakes. The 1994 version had rubber brake lines.

under the fuel tank. Some 1994 916 SPs also came with a carbon-fibre airbox, but – in typical fashion – this wasn't universal. As with all previous SPs, the front 320mm disc brakes were fully floating cast iron, and, in an effort to improve braking performance, the brake pads changed to Ferodo 450. The weight was down to 192kg, and, with a top speed of 270km/h, the 916 SP brilliantly upheld the performance tradition of the earlier Sport Production series. Like the 916 Strada, production of the 1994 916 SP was at the Cagiva factory in Varese, and, to justify the high price, each SP came with a race stand and red motorcycle cover. The 1994 916 SP was also affected by a recall, in early 1997, to replace the rear wheel spindle and hub bearing. In the manner of earlier Ducatis, the individual specification of the 916 SP was often inconsistent, this also being evident through 1995. It was almost as if the 916 SP was being built as a limited edition using parts that were available at the time. Also, compared to the 916 Strada, the performance of the 916 SP barely lived up to the claims. The German magazine *PS*, in August 1994, achieved 259km/h from its test machine, only a few km/h up on the standard 916.

For 1995, the 916 SP was virtually unchanged, although there was a predictable slight lowering in specification. Historically, this had often been a feature of Ducatis, but, fortunately, the 916 SP remained largely as before, even if the machine was marginally less suited to racing duties. The biggest changes were to the electrical system, with small alterations to the wiring, and the inclusion of an external power module and 15-amp fuse to protect the ignition and injection system relay. Even the type of fuses and connectors varied depending on the individual machine. Whereas the 916 Biposto received the new 1.6M CPU, the 916 SP, still with twin injectors, retained the earlier P8 system with a separate rpm sensor. Inside the engine, the titanium conrods became normal Pankl steel, as fitted to the Senna, despite information to the contrary supplied in the official workshop manual. While heavier than the titanium type, the steel rods were also known to fail. Some 1995 916 SPs also had a drilled clutch basket, but this also wasn't universal. As had happened during 1994, the specification would often depend on what was available on the day that that particular machine was assembled.

Cosmetically, the 1995 916 SP was almost indistinguishable from the 1994 version, and, as with other 1995 models, the fairing was retained by screws rather than rivets. Screws retained most of the fairing screens, but this wasn't consistent.

Although the brakes were unchanged, the 1995 916 SP had stainless steel brake lines and Frendo brake pads. The frame was reinforced and now constructed of ALS 450 tubing, and there was an extended carbon-fibre chain cover. Production for 1995 was back at Borgo Panigale, but the production numbers were still very limited. Only 401 916 SPs were manufactured in 1995, coincidentally an identical figure to the number of legendary 1974 750 Super Sports. The 916 SP may not have been as unique as the original 750 Super Sport, but it still epitomised the very best in race-bred sporting motorcycling. With the individual specification of each 916 SP seemingly slightly different, it also upheld a quaint Ducati tradition.

The 916 SP became the SP3 for 1996, now with

a numbered plaque on the top triple clamp, similar to those that had graced all the earlier 888 Sport Productions. The engine specifications remained as for 1995 (still with steel H-section conrods), and, by now, there seemed to be a little more consistency in the general specification. There was also the new series of crankcases without the earlier kickstart boss; the SP3 crankcases also featuring 102mm (up from 100mm) cylinder mouths, allowing the easy installation of a 96mm bore to give 955cc. There was even less carbon-fibre on the SP3, with the clutch cover now aluminium, and the exhaust pipe insulating panel plastic. As with the earlier 916 SP, production was also limited, and only 497 SP3s were produced. Initial press releases for the 1997 model year indicated the 916 SP would be available for a further year but this proved not to be the case.

Also during 1996, a small number (54) of 955cc SPAs (Sport Production America) were produced as homologation specials for AMA Superbike racing. AMA homologation requirements were such that 50 examples of a production machine sharing its displacement with the racer needed to be imported into the US. Thus the SPA was essentially an SP3 with a 955cc engine. Changes included a 96mm cylinder and piston, lighter crankshaft with Pankl H-section titanium conrods, revised final drive gearing, and different lighting. The IAW twin injector system was still a P8, but with a 070 EPROM. In all other respects, the engine and chassis specifications were as the 916 SP3, and there was little to tell them apart. The fairing decals were still '916,' though the engine came with ZDM955 engine numbers. The SPA was the only production street Ducati to come with a 955cc engine and, thus, was quite unique. However, despite claims that this would be one of the most collectable of all street 916s, the appearance of the 916 SPS in 1997 trumped it. The 916 SPS was an even higher specification machine, and provided better overall performance.

Distinguishing the 916 SP from the regular 916 was an Öhlins rear shock absorber, and carbon-fibre chainguard.

From 1995, the 916 for Europe was generally a Biposto with a steel rear subframe and passenger footpegs. This lasted virtually unchanged through until 1998.

recalled to replace the rear wheel spindle, along with the roller bearing and seals on the right side of the eccentric hub. The new spindle was an improved design, being oversized on the right end.

When it came to performance, the 916 didn't disappoint. The mid-range power was noticeably stronger than that of the 888 Strada, and, because the overall machine was smaller and more aerodynamic, the performance approached that of the earlier high specification Sport Production 888s. The early production versions seemed especially fast, as evidenced by *Moto Sprint* in its test of an early 916. It managed a top speed of 255.1km/h and a standing start 400m time of 10.68 seconds at 207.410km/h. This was faster than all 888 SPs except the 888 SPS and SP5. Where the 916 really departed from the earlier 888 was in its racetrack prowess, and comparison tests around the world lauded the 916 as the most racing-orientated sports bike available. As tested by *Motorcyclist* magazine

in September 1996, the rear wheel power of 103.4 horsepower at 9000rpm may not have been class leading, but the 916 provided superior racetrack capability than any 600, 750, or open-class Japanese sports bike. The only compromise was street comfort.

After only one year, the 916 Strada evolved into the 916 Biposto (dual seat). Apart from the dual seat, the main development for 1995 was the replacement of the P8 CPU with a new, smaller, 1.6 M unit. Designed specifically for single injectors (though it would later also be adapted for twin injectors operating simultaneously), this also saw revisions to the sensors and pickups, along with a different 061 EPROM. The earlier separate power modules were now incorporated inside the computer, and there was a new, more waterproof relay with a separate 15-amp fuse. The P8 system required an individual injection timing sensor to detect the phase (from the half-speed timing belt drive jackshaft) and an rpm sensor (recognising four tabs on the crankshaft

Fortunately, the addition of a dual seat did little to detract from the 916's fine lines. This is a 1997 version with adjustable brake and clutch levers.

flywheel), a single sensor (from the timing belt jackshaft) replacing these. This read the 46 teeth and a slot of two teeth. Unfortunately, this system wasn't quite as effective as that of the earlier P8, as the jackshaft gear was susceptible to developing mechanical backlash. Thus, if there was any looseness in the gear drive, the computer (calculating ignition advance and rpm from a sophisticated acceleration/deceleration algorithm) would become confused and a misfire could develop, particularly on a steady throttle. Along with the revised injection system came a new alternator and regulator, these being fitted from engine number 002879 (frame number 002470).

To allow for the inclusion of the dual seat, the frame was reinforced and the rear subframe was steel. The frame, too, was now of ALS 450 tubing rather than the earlier 25CrMo 4. In addition to the associated footpeg brackets, there was a longer chain cover, and, to accommodate the extra weight, the 916 Biposto received a new Showa GD052-007-50 rear shock absorber. The only real downside to the dual seat was an additional weight penalty, the dry weight increasing to 204kg. Hardly the most effective or comfortable two-seater, this adaptation was significant, and very important for sales. Potential buyers often found it easier to justify their purchase if there was provision to take a partner for an occasional ride, at least, albeit a short and uncomfortable one.

There were also a few smaller developments for 1995. Problems with the fairing interfering with the side-mounted battery on some 1994 models saw an additional rubber protection pad inside the fairing for the 1995 model year. The fairing and screen fastening system was revised, too, for 1995, with screws replacing the earlier rivets. In an effort to improve front braking performance, Ferodo Ferit I/D 450 FF brake pads replaced the Fren-do. From frame number 003766, there was a recall to install a modified sidestand spring plate, followed by another recall to replace the throttle cable (up until frame number 005054). Despite these small improvements, what was really evident was that the 916 Biposto was being downgraded slightly and made more economical to produce. This had been a feature of Ducatis in the past, and had continued under the Cagiva regime. The 1.6 M injection system was undoubtedly cheaper to produce, as were the forged steel conrods. Fortunately, this scenario would change after 1996, with the injection of funds from the Texas Pacific Group. While economics were an undoubted concern, competition within the marketplace and a goal to increase production and sales ensured that each year saw an improved model. The 916 Biposto, however, wasn't quite as strong a performer as the 1994 Monoposto. *Moto Sprint* achieved a top speed of 253.8km/h with a standing start 400m time of 10.96 seconds at 201.5km/h.

As has often been the case throughout the history of Ducati production, the US received slightly different versions of the 916. Whereas elsewhere the Biposto replaced the 1994 916 Monoposto, for 1995 the US version was still a solo seater. US versions were, thus, similar in specification to the Senna but for a regular 916 Biposto engine without the Pankl conrods. The frame featured an aluminium rear subframe, and, in response to stateside complaints about the rebound damping of the Showa shock absorber, there was an Öhlins DU 3420 rear shock.

Production problems throughout 1995 saw demand for the 916 continue unabated, so it wasn't surprising that there were few changes for the 1996 model year. After all, the factory 955 racer had proven unbeatable in World Superbike, and the 916 was still unquestionably the most desirable production sporting motorcycle available. Thus, for 1996 there were only a small number of changes. The clutch cover incorporated sound absorption material, and the fairing, sound deadening panels. There were also new

crankcases without the kickstart boss and a stronger locating system. Four M8 x 90mm screws replaced the previous M8 x 75 and 85mm screws and there was a total of 16 retaining screws rather than the previous 14. Although factory press sheets claimed that, for 1996, the clutch and brake levers would be adjustable, as with the 916 SP and Senna, this didn't happen until the 1997 model year. During November 1996, all earlier 916s (and 748s) were recalled to lubricate the throttle control linkage pin. This affected machines until frame number 008150 (000711 for France). Only a few months later (in July 1997), this recall was extended to include 916s to frame number 010985 (001012 for France). Also affecting those 916s until 010985 was another safety recall, after some failure of the roller bearings and seals in the eccentric rear hub.

There were few changes to the 916 Biposto for 1997. Production had been dramatically reduced during 1996, as large numbers of motorcycles lay unfinished at Bologna, waiting for the supply of vital spare parts. This had seen production of the 916 range drop to only 2896 that year, and, as there was still considerable demand, the model continued virtually unchanged. Just as they had been since 1994, the 916 was only available in red. Although the 916 Monoposto with Öhlins rear shock absorber was still available in the US, buyers there could now also opt for the 916 Biposto (with steel rear subframe and Showa shock). The 916 Monoposto was also available in limited numbers in France (100) and Japan (25) for 1997.

After originally being specified for 1996, the 916 for the 1997 model year received adjustable brake and clutch levers. Also for 1997, there were new specification front brake calipers, these being fitted from serial number 010082 (000963 for France). Soon afterwards, there were new 320mm stainless steel front brake discs (from number 010233). While looking very similar to previous discs, these now had a different spring loading system to provide smoother operation. During 1997, a Japanese Shindengen regulator finally replaced the troublesome Ducati Energia. This was still mounted on the right side of the

continued on page 48

The Senna

Also for 1995 was the first of the limited edition 916 Senna models. A friend of the Castiglionis, the great Formula One racing driver Ayrton Senna was a Ducati enthusiast. Senna had been Formula One World Champion in 1988, 1990, and 1991, and, on March 7 1994, had visited the Ducati factory in Bologna and approved a variant of the 916 to carry his name. This was originally to be launched at the Monaco Formula One Grand Prix in May, but was delayed due to Senna's death. On 8 May 1994, Senna died at the Formula One race at Imola, only a short distance from Bologna. After persuading Senna's widow Viviane to proceed with the model as a tribute, the 916 Senna appeared for the 1995 model year. Production was scheduled for 300 units, with the profits going to the Senna Foundation to support infant charity programmes in Brazil and around the world. Distinguished by its black and

grey colour scheme accentuated by red wheels, the Senna was an amalgam of the 916 Strada and SP. The engine specifications were as for the 1994 916 Strada, but updated with the 1.6 M CPU. Thus, the Senna engine featured steel Pankl conrods, and, with single injectors, produced 109bhp at 9000rpm. The chassis came from the 916 SP. With only a solo seat, there was an aluminium rear subframe, an Öhlins DU 3420 rear shock absorber, and fully floating cast iron 320mm front brake discs. Also shared with the SP were adjustable brake and clutch levers, stainless steel brake lines, and several carbon-fibre parts. These included the front mudguard, clutch cover, chainguard, and exhaust pipe insulating panel.

For 1996, another version was proposed, the Senna II. This was to be very similar to the 1995 model but for an aluminium clutch cover and plastic

Although not providing SP performance or exclusivity, the Senna offered an imitable style. Here is the first Senna of 1995.

The second series of Senna, the 1997 Senna II, came in a lighter shade of silver, but still with red wheels.

exhaust pipe insulation panel. The main identifying feature was to be yellow wheels, but production problems during 1996 meant that there was no Senna II that year. Senna's brother-in-law, Flavio Lalli, died after crashing one of the first 916 Sennas in March 1996, this further curtailing interest in the series from the Senna Foundation.

It was only after the agreement with the Texas Pacific Group in September 1996 that the production problems ended, and another run of 916 Sennas was sanctioned. When these appeared, they were a lighter grey than before, with red, rather than yellow, wheels. The number of Senna IIs produced in 1997 was similar to the first Senna, with 301 units manufactured. The final version of the Senna appeared for 1998, now black, with the new Vignelli logos. Distinguishing the 1998 Senna were, as before, a number of carbon-fibre body parts (front mudguard, chainguard and licence plate bracket), Öhlins rear suspension unit, and a numbered plaque. Further distinguishing the 1998 model was a carbon-fibre airbox (as with the 916 SPS) and exhaust heat shield. As previously, production was 300 for 1998, but they were slow

sellers. The final new Senna was auctioned at the World Ducati Weekend 2000 at Misano. Ultimately, the problem with the Senna was that too many were produced for it to have real limited edition status. Also, with no exotic engine components, the Senna was little more than an overpriced 916 Monoposto. Compared to a 916 SP (and especially a 916 SPS), it represented poor value for money.

A final series of Senna was constructed for 1998, now black, with new Vignelli logos and a numbered plaque on the top triple clamp.

engine, underneath the battery, and promised to finally overcome the regulator problems that had plagued the 916 since its inception.

In early 1997, a Bosch fuel pump replaced the Walbro that had been fitted to all four-valve Ducatis (851 and 888) since 1992. The Bosch fuel pump became standard fitment on the 916 after serial number 010532 (000963 for France), but it wasn't initially totally satisfactory, and there were fuel supply problems experienced, when the fuel level was low, or at extremely high temperatures. To rectify this, the deflector and fuel pump mount were modified from serial number 012391 (001092 for France). Although it was undoubtedly an improvement, the Bosch pump (made in both Germany and the Czech Republic) was also unreliable and prone to failure. Further problems surfaced during 1997, when it was found that a small number of engines had insufficiently torqued cylinder heads. This affected the 916 Biposto (USA) from engine number 011011 to 011260, and the 916 Biposto (Europe) from engine number 011299 to 011460. These small problems aside, with 1997 production nearly doubling from 1996, to 5281 units, the 916 still set the standard for desirability in production sporting motorcycles. One of the strangest problems occurred in Australia, where it was found that the unique 916 twin headlight arrangement failed to pass strict Australian Design Rules that forbid only one headlight to operate on low beam. This saw all 916s (and 748s) in Australia being recalled to install an alternative fairing with an incredibly ugly locally-designed square headlight. Although very few owners agreed to the recall request, this problem meant that all new 916s and 748s had to be sold with the square headlight until the standard headlight and electrical system were modified for the 1999 model year.

Even then, although it was into its fourth production year, the 916 beat off challenge from the competition. It had taken the Japanese manufacturers some time to rise to the 916 challenge, but, during 1997, both Honda and Suzuki offered competitive 1000cc 90° V-twins: the VTR1000F and TL1000S. However, on the racetrack, the 916 remained unsurpassed. In a *Cycle World* comparison test in April 1997, a 916 turned the fastest lap times ever for a production motorcycle at Willow Springs – and this was straight out of the box, with minimal suspension adjustment. Despite lower peak power than the Honda or Suzuki, the 916 also posted the highest top speed of 154.7mph (249km/h). As summed up by *Cycle World*, "If that doesn't earn the right to the sportbike throne, what does? The king ain't dead – in fact he's not even breathing hard."

By the 1998 model year, the influence of the new ownership of Ducati was more evident. Not only was there a change in corporate policy, in a world driven by market forces there were now visible changes to all models from year to year. Whereas the 916 had remained in production virtually unchanged for three years, small details now set the 1998 916 Biposto apart from earlier versions. The most obvious difference concerned the Vignelli new logos: there no longer being a 'DUCATI' on the fuel tank. This minimalist look came in for some criticism and it was no surprise to see a reversal of this change for 1999. As with all 1998 models, there was a Shindengen regulator, and no battery charge light on the dashboard. While the Shindengen regulator may not have looked particularly aesthetic, it proved to be far more reliable than the earlier regulator. Engine developments saw improved Kevlar-reinforced timing belts, as fitted to the racing 916. Also, along with the braided steel front brake lines came similar clutch and rear brake lines. With yellow 916 Bipostos now available alongside red, there was a small

continued on page 53

48

The 916 SPS (1997-98)

Undoubtedly the most significant new model for Ducati for the 1997 model year was the 916 SPS (Sport Production Special). Although still continuing the tradition of the Sport Production series by being a homologation special, this was an even more impressive machine than the 916 SP. There was also more to the 916 SPS than merely a larger engine than its predecessor. The general level of specification and performance made it one of the most desirable Ducatis ever. In the past, the only SPS had been the imposing 888 SPS of 1992, this being essentially a street 888 SP with a full race-spec Corsa engine. The 916 SPS continued this tradition admirably.

Reliability problems with the racing 996 during 1996 required a new set of stronger crankcases be homologated for the 1997 racing season, which led to production of a 996cc Sport Production series. Continuing an unusual tradition of naming models

by the line-up code rather than actual capacity, this was still titled a 916. The biggest changes occurred in the engine, the revised crankcases now having a 105mm crankcase mouth with the cylinder studs spaced 123mm apart rather than the previous 120mm. With a wider cylinder stud placement, this meant the cylinder liners could now be a more generous (3.5mm) thick. To allow for the larger cylinders, there were smaller diameter (M6 x 80mm) screws at the crankcase mouth; the total number of crankcase retaining screws was 16.

Complementing the larger engine was a redesigned cylinder head. There were larger inlet valves (36mm) and larger inlet ports, though the exhaust valves remained at 30mm. From the racing programme came new desmodromic camshafts that were designed to improve mid-range power at the expense of the top-end. The inlet camshaft provided less valve lift than the 916 SP (10.8mm), along with

Still titled a 916, there was little to distinguish the 916 SPS visually from the previous 916 SP. However, the 996c engine provided considerably more performance and the carbon-fibre exhaust shields hid a larger diameter exhaust system.

less duration. The inlet valve opened 14° before top dead centre, closing 73° after bottom dead centre. The exhaust camshaft provided more valve lift (9.8mm), and opened the valve 57° before bottom dead centre, closing 23° after top dead centre. The individually balanced crankshaft was lighter, and featured Pankl H-section conrods. The new 98mm pistons had a very low deck height (27.4mm) and provided a slightly increased compression ratio of 11.5:1. The electronic injection system was the twin injector P8, as before, but with a 071 EPROM, and the throttle bodies remained 50mm in diameter.

What was different, though, was the exhaust system, this now having 50mm header pipes. With Termignoni mufflers, power was a claimed 134bhp at the crankshaft, at 10,500rpm. Later, this figure was revised to 123bhp at 9500rpm, though with no apparent changes in specification. While the ultimate power of the 916 SPS wasn't much more than that of the 916 SP, the power delivery was much improved, this being less peaky and frenetic. Other developments on the 916 SPS included new straight-cut primary gears, these being the 32/59 toothed gears (1.84:1) from the 1996 916 Racing. This, too, would solve one of the problems that had plagued powerful Ducati engines with the earlier 31/62 primary gears. Because there was no hunting

tooth with the 2:1 ratio to spread the load evenly, they were known to fail in extreme circumstances. There was also a different gearbox for the 916 SPS, this having the same closer ratios as the 748. Because third to sixth gears were closer than before, a 15-tooth gearbox sprocket raised the final drive over the 916 SP.

The general chassis was identical to that of the 916 SP, although for the 1997 model year the Brembo front brake calipers were improved. Thus, with 916 decals there was little to differentiate the two models, only the '916 SPS' plaque on the top triple clamp and the carbon-fibre exhaust shield giving the larger machine away. On the road, however, the 916 SPS again set the standard for street bike performance. As tested by the Italian magazine *Motociclismo* in April 1997, the 916 SPS achieved 270.1km/h, or 275.4km/h with the optional Termignoni mufflers and alternative EPROM. The standing start 400m time was 10.841 (10.543) seconds at a speed of 220.6 (223.2km/h). The 1997 916 SPS was also produced in fewer numbers than the later versions, with only 404 manufactured. In line with other 916s, there was also a recall, to lubricate the throttle control linkage, and roller bearings and seals in the eccentric rear hub, this affecting the 916 SPS up to frame number 000363.

Minimalism in logo design took over for 1998, and there was no decal on the tank this year. The 916 SPS featured new forks with wider brake caliper mounts, and inside the 996cc engine were titanium conrods.

From serial number 000235, there was a Bosch fuel pump, which also incorporated modifications to the deflector and mount, from number 000521 (1998 model year). However, while the Bosch pump was an improvement, there were still problems.

The 916 SPS was again offered for 1998, now with the new, minimalist Vignelli logos, but still titled a 916 rather than a 996. There was no 'DUCATI' badge on the tank this year, and the big change in the 916 SPS for 1998 was a vast increase in the number produced, to 1058. The numbered plaque on the top triple clamp now incorporated four digits, further diluting exclusivity. However, although it may not have been quite as select as in 1997, the 916 SPS for 1998 did incorporate some improvements. The general engine specifications were unchanged, though there were new titanium conrods and revised valve rocker arms from developments on the World Superbike racers. The conrods were no longer the Pankl H-section as before, but they were still Pankl, being similar in shape to the regular forged 916 Biposto conrod, and were also shared with the 748 SPS. The weight of these titanium conrods was 395g: not quite as light as the H-section titanium, but still considerably lighter than even the H-section steel conrod.

As the 916 SPS was still primarily a homologation model for World Superbike racing, there was a new frame, visually identical to before, but made of lighter 25CrMo4 steel tubing of thinner section. This was done to give the racer a less rigid chassis, so as not to magnify suspension problems, but would be barely noticeable on a street motorcycle. After many years of waiting, the airbox was finally now of carbon-fibre, bringing with it the claimed benefits of increased chassis rigidity.

The rest of the chassis was as before, although the Showa front forks were new, the lower sliders having wider front brake caliper mounts. This also saw a new gold-series Brembo front brake caliper. While these forks and brakes were only shared with the 748 SPS for 1998, they would eventually make it to all production Ducatis. Though an improvement as street equipment, the downside was that the wider brake caliper mounts couldn't accommodate any aftermarket racing Brembo calipers without an adaptor plate. Other improvements for 1998 included an Öhlins steering damper, and additional carbon-fibre heat shields and panels. In line with all 1998 model year Ducatis, there was a Shindengen regulator, and no battery charge light incorporated on the dashboard. There was a recall early in 1998, from frame number 000437 to 000689, to replace unsuitable fuel lines inside the fuel tank.

The only model indication on the 1998 916 SPS was a small decal at the rear. This still carried a 916 designation, despite the 996cc engine.

From December 1997, and frame number 001169, modified airboxes were fitted. As with the 916 Biposto, the recalls continued throughout 1998. From frame number 001061 to 001186, there was a recall to tighten the primary drive gear, presumably loose in assembly, and, from 000440 to 001368, a recall to replace the shim between the lower roller and circlip on the timing layshaft. In November 1999, all 916 SPSs from frame number 000001 to 001728 were recalled to have the rear wheel axle checked for possible defects.

Ducati under its new management could have been criticised for increasing production of the 916 SPS to new levels for an SP series. The 916 SPS (and earlier 916 SP) had received much praise in the motorcycle press and, by increasing the production, the previous exclusivity was no longer guaranteed. However, while the numbers produced for 1998 were higher, the specification wasn't lowered, and the 916 SPS remained at the forefront of production sports bike performance. This was evidenced when tested by *Sportbike* magazine in the US. With 118.2 horsepower at 9500rpm, the 1998 916 SPS went through the quarter mile in 10.43 seconds at 134.48mph (216km/h). The measured top speed was 165mph (265.5km/h).

Also during 1998, a limited run of Fogarty Replica 916 SPSs was built so as to homologate a revised frame for World Superbike. Although it only featured a change to the rear bracing tube to increase the airbox volume, this was an extremely successful modification. The 202 machines were available only in England, and while they were virtually identical to regular 916 SPS, there were a few extra touches to ensure exclusivity and justify the premium price. The decals were patterned on the Ducati Performance 996 World Superbike racer of Carl Fogarty, and the wheels were black five-spoke Marchesini rather than the regular gold three-spoke Brembo. The fuel tank, bike cover, and key fob also came with a Fogarty signature. Other features specific to the Fogarty Replica included a titanium exhaust system, and a carbon-fibre seat unit with racing Tecnosel seat pad. So successful was the limited edition Fogarty version, that there was another series produced for 1999, and 2000 (see Chapter Six: The 996). This time, the Fogarty Replica was available outside England, but still not in the US.

In order to homologate a revised frame and airbox for World Superbike racing, a small number of these Fogarty Replicas were produced for the British market during 1998. Upgraded specifications included racing decals and Marchesini wheels.

Many US specification 916s offered differed to those in Europe. This 1998 US 916 is a Monoposto, and has an Öhlins rear shock absorber.

Many US specification 916s offered differed to those in Europe. This 1998 US 916 is a Monoposto, and has an Öhlins rear shock absorber.

increase in production for 1998, and the total numbers produced of the 916 family was 5460. Red was still the most popular: production favouring the traditional colour by around three to one. Although the general form of the 916s was still a Biposto, a very small number of Monoposto versions were also available in France (8), and Japan (45). The 1998 US 916 was still either a Biposto (with Showa shock absorber), or Monoposto (with an Öhlins shock absorber). Unlike Europe, both US versions still had rubber brake lines, and more Monoposto versions were built. From November 1998, the Monoposto saddle was also available as an option for all Bipostos, coming with a complete kit that included the taillight and wiring.

After several years in production, it was surprising to see several safety recalls during this period. This reduction in quality control

could have been tied to the rapid increase in production levels, but, to its credit, the Ducati technical department acted on problems immediately. Following the recall of 1994 916 Monopostos, in April 1997, to replace the rear wheel spindle, along with the roller bearing and seals on the right side of the eccentric hub, this was extended in November 1997 to encompass some later machines. Now the 916 from 013850 to 013980 (001034 to 001044 for France) were included in this recall. From December 1997, the airbox material was altered on all 916 Bipostos, the modified airbox being fitted from frame number 013274 (001093 for France). In early 1998, there was also a recall to replace the fuel lines inside the fuel tank. This affected the 916 from frame number 011992 to 012392. Apparently, this batch of motorcycles had fuel

Living with a 916

There is no doubt that the 916 has been the most successful single model in Ducati's history. Despite a long production run it is still lauded as representing the epitome of sporting motorcycling. But does the image live up to the reality? In a survey conducted by Don Sucher of Ducatis Unlimited Connection (a US-based internet site) during 1999, 96% of respondents indicated they were exceptionally pleased with their 916. However, more than half reported electrical problems (other than the battery). There is no doubt that the introduction of Japanese electrical components has been beneficial to the reliability of items such as the regulator and alternator. Other complaints concerned the brakes and the difficulty in finding neutral.

Engine problems were mainly confined to the clutch (leaking seals in the master and slave cylinders), and clutch basket wear. Some cases of the inner timing belt cover locating nut loosening and falling off were reported, this leading to catastrophic engine failure as the nut lodged under the camshaft belt causing it to break. Other small problems included fuel system failures, coolant leaks, cracked coolant expansion chambers, and oil leaks from the engine cases. It was significant that 53% of owners of 1998 models reported no problems, this indicating that quality was improving under TPG. In Europe, particularly Germany with its unrestricted autobahns, engine failure has been more prevalent. Main bearing failure has led to crankcase cracking, even on post-1996 versions, and eventually the crankshaft breaking in extreme circumstances. Other problems have been the airbox breaking, and fuel pump failure.

As an unabashed single purpose machine, living with a 916 undoubtedly means a sacrifice in comfort. This not only includes the extremely sporting riding position, but also the heat emanating from the exhaust pipes, hard seat, and strong clutch pull. As a racing inspired design, service intervals are more regular than on other motorcycles. And with the high revving nature of the engine timing belt maintenance and regular replacement is essential. Aftermarket higher rise handlebars

are obtainable, and there is also a wide range of performance and lightweight parts available so as to individually craft a 916. No motorcycle is perfect but for its intended purpose the 916 takes a lot of beating.

Although often a little extreme for street duties, the 916 is a perfect companion for the trend of the 1990s: racetrack ride days. As a racing-inspired design, the 916 excels on the track, and can be ridden to its limits in safety – and without fear of the constabulary.

A line up of 916s, with a 1997 Biposto at the front. Behind are two more Bipostos and a Senna II.

lines installed that were unsuitable for this application. From frame number 013196 to 014145 there was a further 916 Biposto recall to tighten the primary drive gear. There was an even more serious recall in June 1998, this affecting all versions of the 916 from 1994 until 1997: some higher mileage examples had experienced the alternator nut on the crankshaft loosening, the result being that the washer behind the flywheel dislodged and fell between the inner ring and the flywheel gear. The recalls continued through 1998, when it was found that the shim placed between the lower roller and the circlip on the timing layshaft could fail, leading to severe engine damage. 916 Bipostos from serial number 011993 to 014893 (001094 to 001186 fro France) were recalled to have this shim replaced. Following a fatal accident in Germany, attributed to rear wheel axle failure on a 916, all 916s from frame number 000001 until 015095 (000001 to 001207 for France) were recalled, in November 1999, to have the rear axle tested ultrasonically.

Up until 1998, the 916 had really only undergone minor evolutionary development. The essential motorcycle was virtually identical to the first model of 1994, and, such was the excellence of the design, demand was strong, and it was still highly competitive on the racetrack. Yet, by now, the 916 was coming under more competition in the marketplace from other manufacturers. With the imminent availability of the Aprilia RSV Mille, the 916 needed to be updated to meet the challenge. And, while it could still be argued that the 916 continued to be aesthetically and dynamically superior to its rivals, it needed more capacity,

and a power increase, to meet this competition head on. This was admirably achieved for the 1999 model year with the 996. More than simply a big-bore 916, the new 996 represented the next major evolution of one of the greatest ever motorcycle designs.

The 748

With production problems seemingly solved (at least temporarily), at Borgo Panigale, the 916 range was expanded considerably for the 1995 model year. Not only was there the limited edition 916 Senna, but there were three smaller versions: the 748 (Strada and Biposto) and the 748 SP (Sport Production). The 748 Strada (with a solo seat) and Biposto were intended as entry level 916s, though they were still hardly budget machines. For most markets in 1995, only the Biposto was available, although a small number of monoposto Stradas (120) were built for France that year. The 748 SP was a solo-seat homologation machine, specifically for the expanding class of Supersport racing. Here, production 600cc four-cylinder motorcycles were pitted against 750cc twins and, just as the 955 had proved that a twin could mix it with and beat the smaller fours, Ducati hoped the 748 would repeat this in the production-based Supersport class.

When it came to selecting the bore and stroke for the 748, there was an historical precedent for choosing 88 x 61.5mm. The first four-valve engine, back in 1986, had been a 748 with those engine dimensions, these in turn coming from the earlier two-valve 750 F1. However, apart from the bore and stroke, the 748 was based on the large crankcase six-speed engine, rather than the smaller five-speed crankcase that remained the preserve of the two-valve 750 and 600 Supersport. In most other respects, the engine of the 748 Strada

Apart from the fairing decals, there was nothing to distinguish the 748 from the 916. The outright performance was also surprisingly similar.

and Biposto was similar in specification to the 916 Biposto for 1995. Although the cylinder heads were new, the camshafts were the same, as were the valve sizes of 33mm and 29mm. Also shared with the 916 Biposto was the Weber electronic injection system with a single injector per cylinder and a 1.6 M CPU, though the throttle body was reduced in size to 44mm. The crankshaft featured regular forged conrods, and the flywheel was lighter on the 748. Unlike the 916, there was no external oil filter (reducing the oil capacity from four to three-and-a-half litres). The 748 also received the closer ratio gearbox of the 888 SP5, with different third (28/20), fourth (26/22), fifth (24/23), and sixth gears (23/24) to those of the 916. With a compression ratio of 11.5:1, and a 45mm exhaust system, the resulting 748 engine produced 98bhp at 11,000rpm. This wasn't much less than a 916, and the specific power output of the 748 at 131bhp/litre was the highest yet attained by Ducati for a series production machine. The power delivery was also quite different, the 748 requiring considerably more revs to attain a similar level of performance to the 916. Thus, it was even more important that the timing belt tension was correctly maintained, and the belts changed at regular intervals.

The chassis of the 748 was virtually identical to that of the 916. Both models used a frame constructed of ALS 450 tubing, also both offering a variable steering head angle. As with the 916 Biposto, the 748 Biposto received a steel rear subframe, along with a dual seat. The 748 Strada chassis followed that of the 1994 916 Strada (and US models) by retaining the aluminium rear subframe. Because of the necessity for the Biposto to accommodate a passenger, both models also featured slightly different Showa rear suspension. These were identical to those units on the 916 Strada and Biposto (a GD052-007-02 for the Strada and

GD052-007-50 for the Biposto). The 43mm Showa GD 051 forks were the same as those on the 916.

The Brembo wheels and brakes, too, were identical to those on the 916 Biposto. Thus, the 748 was also afflicted with marginal braking, the 320mm stainless steel brake discs, gold series Brembo P4.30/34 calipers, and rubber brake lines contributing to a soft-feeling system. In line with the 1995 916, the 748 received Ferodo Ferit I/D 450 FF brake pads. The main basic chassis change was the use of a lower profile front tyre (120/60 ZR17), a smaller (180/55 ZR17) rear tyre, and a narrower drive chain, this being a DID 520 VL4 ($\frac{5}{8}$ x $\frac{1}{4}$in). Along with the different engine (less reciprocating weight) and power characteristics, the lower profile front and smaller rear tyre provided different steering and handling to the 916. Many, including Ducati's official tester, Andrea Forni, claimed the 748 to be a superior handler, at least on the street. Visually, there was little to set the red 748 Strada and Biposto apart from the 916. At 200kg for the Strada and 202kg for the Biposto, the 748 also provided astonishing performance for a 750cc twin. The Italian magazine *Motociclismo*, in June 1995 achieved a top speed of 249.6km/h, with a standing start 400m time of 11.6 seconds at 193.5km/h. As production of the 748 commenced after the 916 had been in production for some time, most of the early problems had been resolved. From frame number 000095, there was a recall to install a modified sidestand spring plate. As with the 916, there was another recall to replace the throttle cable, this affecting the first 1237 machines. Generally, too, the 748 wasn't quite as popular as the 916, and a total of 2558 (Biposto, Strada and SP) were produced in 1995.

For the 1996 model year, the only change to the 748 Biposto was the incorporation of a sound-deadening clutch cover and the new

continued on page 62

The 748 SP and 748 SPS

Joining the 748 Strada and Biposto for 1995 was the 748 SP, this being primarily a homologation special for Supersport racing. However, although it carried the 'Sport Production' designation, the 748 SP was a lower specification machine than its larger, 916 SP, brother. What really set the 748 SP apart was the striking yellow bodywork, with its white number plate on the solo seat, and, in 1995, the 748 SP couldn't be confused with any other four-valve Ducati.

The engine specifications were little changed from those of the 748 Strada and Biposto. The compression ratio was a touch higher than the regular 748, at 11.6:1, and the camshafts different. While the exhaust camshaft was the same as that of the 916 SP, there was a new inlet camshaft, this having timing figures similar to those of the 851 SP, but with more valve lift (10.87mm). Unlike the 916 SP that featured a P8 CPU with twin injectors per cylinder, the 748 SP shared its single injectors and 1.6 M CPU with the other 748s and 916 Biposto. Setting the 748 SP apart, though, were Pankl H-section steel conrods, as fitted to the Senna and 1994 916 Strada. There was an external oil cooler, and, with a larger diameter exhaust (45mm going to 50mm), power was up to 104bhp, at 11,000rpm.

Engine developments included the timing gear being located on the timing layshaft by an offset Woodruff key to advance the valve timing.

When it came to the chassis, the 748 SP was more like the 916 SP. With only a solo seat, the rear subframe was aluminium, and the suspension upgraded to include an Öhlins DU 3420 rear shock absorber. The front brakes, too, were considerably improved over those of the 748 Strada and Biposto with 320mm fully floating cast iron discs, stainless steel brake lines, and an adjustable lever. The drive chain was the narrower 520 item, as with all 748s. Unlike the 916 SP, however, there were no carbon-fibre body parts, although there were carbon-fibre Termignoni mufflers. There was no doubt that the striking 748 SP was an immediate success. However, while weighing only 198kg, the 748 SP didn't offer any more performance than a 748 Biposto, at least in standard trim. In a test by the German magazine *Motorrad*, in April 1995, the 748 SP achieved 248km/h. The 748 SP was also a reasonably limited edition motorcycle, with only 600 manufactured during 1995.

As it was intended to be raced in 600 Supersport competition, three stages of racing uprating kit were available for the 748 SP. Engine Kit No 1

Resplendent in bright yellow, there was no confusing the 748 SP with its larger brother. Specific 748 SP features were the solo seat with white patch, and cast iron brake discs.

The 748 SPS replaced the 748 SP for 1998, but, apart from new decals, looked very similar. This is an example of the 1999 version (with tank decals), and was the final model to feature cast iron front brake discs.

included lighter replacement engine parts, such as the clutch and alternator that could be installed without removing the engine from the frame. Engine Kit No 2 included a lighter crankshaft and gearbox selector drum, while the Frame Kit included a replacement fairing, seat, exhaust, injection unit supports, and modified wiring with a lighter generator.

For 1996, there were few changes to the specification of the 748 SP apart from new crankcases (shared with the 748 and 916). Although there was no official factory documentation indicating this, the 748 SP no longer had Pankl conrods, instead receiving the normal forged type. The author noticed this while engines for the 748 SP were being assembled, in September 1996. However, Pankl rods were included in the now-even-more-comprehensive racing uprating kit. Comprising the two engine kits as before, there were now also two frame kits, with an increased range of lightweight components. As a homologation model, the 748 SP was an even more limited production machine than the previous year, with only 400 built. The racing uprating kit for the 748 SP for 1997 comprised only one engine and one frame kit, though these provided a wider range of alternative parts. The engine kit now included replacement valves and valve guides, along with a complete gearbox. The 118-piece frame kit was much as before. A further batch of similar specification 748 SPs were built for 1997, however production was even lower at 305 units. Some of these 1997 models were afflicted with insufficient cylinder head tightening, this affecting the 748 SP from engine number 004793 to 005017. The cylinder heads for 1997 were also the same as the 916 SP, with the cast '4V DOHC' lettering.

Replacing the 748 SP for 1998 was the 748 SPS. This was still a homologation special for 600 Supersport racing and featured a few developments over its predecessor to make it more adaptable in the role as a Supersport racer. Engine developments saw the incorporation of the same forged titanium conrods as used on the 1998 916 SPS, and bronze valve guides. In line with the 916 SPS, there were also new valve rockers. Apart from a front cylinder head with cast lettering, there were no other engine changes. Unlike the 916

SPS, the 748 SPS retained the 31/62 primary drive. There was a new ignition pick-up for track use, and modified voltage regulator. The 748 SPS also received different inlet tracts and throttle bodies, the inlet being incorporated in the throttle body after the throttle valve. The inlet tract was shortened to 33mm, and, while FIM regulations required a maximum 44mm throttle body, early examples of the 748 SPS unfortunately featured throttle bodies with an outside diameter slightly larger than the required 44mm. In March 1998, replacement FIM legal throttle bodies were supplied for racing, although this didn't apply to street machines. At the same time, replacement brake lines were also supplied for racing. There was also a recall on the 748 SPS from frame number 007355 to 007873, during 1998, to tighten the primary drive gear, this not being sufficiently tightened at assembly.

Still only available in yellow, the 748 SPS featured some chassis changes, many of these

being shared with the larger 916 SPS. These included the lighter frame constructed of 25CrMo4, and the new Showa forks with the wider brake caliper mounts. With the new forks came revised Brembo front brake calipers. There was also a braided steel clutch and rear brake line for the 748 SPS. As before, there were the fully floating cast iron front brake discs and Öhlins rear shock absorber, and the weight of the 748 SPS was down slightly to 194kg. As usual, the 748 SPS remained a limited production machine in the line-up, and only 570 were produced for 1998. However, despite the availability of the optional racing uprating kit, the 748 SPS was no longer a competitive prospect for World Supersport racing. For this task, Ducati created a small number of 748 Racing; then offered a complete engine and frame competition kit to transform the 748 SPS to 748 Racing specification. In this form, the 748 SPS remained in the catalogue for 1999, though only 201 were manufactured. A

further three were available for the 2000 model year, but, by now, the 748 SPS was superseded by the more sophisticated 748 R. Unlike the 996 and regular 748 for 1999, the 748 SPS continued virtually unchanged from 1998 but for different graphics. Thus, while all the other Superbikes (Hypersport) now had the 520-watt tri-phase alternator so as to run new headlights, the 748 SPS retained the earlier 350-watt alternator. As a racing homologation machine, this was done in the interest of minimising reciprocating weight, as the older alternator was lighter. In line with the 1999 748 Biposto, the 748 SPS received the new forks and front brake calipers with their wider mounts, although, unlike the 996 SPS, the front brake discs were still the 320mm fully floating cast iron type. The 1999 748 SPS was the final production Ducati with cast iron discs.

There was little to distinguish the 1997 748
Biposto from earlier versions, and, as before, most
were in red.

crankcases. These were shared with the 916
and featured a stronger screw retaining system
and no kickstart boss. Although it was claimed
there would be adjustable brake and clutch
levers, these didn't make it onto the 748 (for
1996 or 1997). There were further problems
with the throttle cable, and, during November
1996, all 748s until frame number 003074 were
recalled to lubricate the throttle control linkage
pin. Soon afterwards, this was extended to
include 748s until frame number 005460.
1996, though, was a very troubled year for
production, with demand far exceeding supply,
and the number of 748s produced (1560) was
down considerably on that of the previous year.

With production levels increasing following
the American TPG buy-in, there was an
additional model offered for 1997: the 748 S.
Initial reports indicated this was a solo-seat
(monoposto) that incorporated the running
gear of the 748 SP with a standard Biposto
engine. At a price similar to the 748 Biposto,
the red or yellow 748 S offered an aluminium
rear subframe, Öhlins shock absorber, fully
floating cast iron front brake discs, along with
a stand and motorcycle cover. It seemed too
good to be true, and, when the production
748 S appeared, it was no surprise to see the
specification downgraded to basically a 748
Biposto with a solo seat. For some reason,
the 748 S wasn't a popular model and very
few were produced. Even compared to the
homologation 748 SP, the 748 S was a very
limited production machine, and only available
in selected European markets. This series of
748 S was only available for 1997, 100 being
manufactured. It was then resurrected for the
2000 model year, when the 748 S became the
middle model in the new three-bike 748 line-up.
This time, though, the 748 S was available as
either Monoposto or Biposto.

There were also only detail changes to the
748 Biposto for 1997. With the order books
overflowing following the production problems

of 1996, and more emphasis placed on getting the ST2 into production, the 748 Biposto was visually identical for yet another year. A small number of yellow versions were produced (44), but red remained the primary colour choice. After some failure of the roller bearings and seals in the eccentric rear hub, there was another safety recall, this affecting all models until frame number 006678. Later, this recall was extended to include a replacement rear wheel spindle, and included 748s from 005769 to 005840 and 008285 to 008519. Further problems surfaced during 1997, when it was found that a small number of engines had insufficiently torqued cylinder heads. This concerned the 748 Biposto from engine number 005018 to 005497. For 1997, there were new specification front brake calipers. These were fitted from serial number 004168. Not long afterwards (from number 004212), there were new brake discs, ostensibly identical but with a new spring loading system. Along with all other models during 1997, the Walbro fuel pump became a Bosch, this being fitted after 748 Biposto serial number 004337. Problems with the fuel delivery in extreme cases saw the Bosch pump deflector and mount being modified, from serial number 006440.

The 748 also made it to the US for 1997, primarily as a yellow solo seat California model. Yet, while it may have looked like a 748 SP, the engine was that of a Biposto (without the external oil cooler), and the rear suspension was Showa. Only a few were produced (190 for California and six for the rest of the US). One was tested by *Motorcyclist* magazine in May 1997. Producing 89.7 horsepower at 10,500rpm, the performance was close to that of a 916, with a best quarter-mile acceleration time of 11.59 seconds at 119.7mph (192.6km/h). The basic problem with the 748 in the US was that, unlike European Supersport regulations, the AMA Supersport rules didn't allow the 748 to compete against the 600cc fours. Thus, the 748 was left out in the wilderness. Unable to compete on the track, and in a land where bigger is always better, the 748 was perceived as a poor relation to the 916.

For the 1998 model year, the 748 was little changed but for the new logos that graced the entire range that year. There were no logos on the fuel tank, only on the fairing, and 1998 saw the adjustable clutch and brake levers first mooted for 1996. There was the new regulator and no longer a battery warning light on the dashboard. Engine developments included the installation of improved Kevlar-reinforced timing belts, these being the same as on the racing versions. As with the 916, a batch of 748s were produced towards the end of 1997 with unsuitable fuel lines inside the fuel tank, and, in early 1998, a recall was issued. This included machines from frame number 006279 to 006961. From December 1997, and frame number 007363, there was a modified airbox (of new material). Also like the 916, there was an even more serious recall in June 1998, this affecting all versions of the 748 from 1995 until 1997. On some machines the alternator nut on the crankshaft had loosened, with the washer behind the flywheel dislodging and falling between the inner ring and the flywheel gear. All 748 Bipostos from frame number 007343 to 007831 were also recalled during 1998, to rectify a possible loose primary drive and oil pump gear. The recalls continued through 1998, when it was found that the shim placed between the lower roller and the circlip on the timing layshaft could fail, leading to severe engine damage. All 748s between engine number 006334 and 008822 were recalled to have this shim replaced.

For the first time, yellow 748 Bipostos were available alongside red in some markets, with

continued on page 67

600 Supersport racing

It wasn't long before the 748 SP emulated the success of its larger brother, the 916 Racing, on the racetrack. During 1995, Belgian rider Michael Paquay rode the Team Alstare 748 SP to victory in the European Supersport Championship, winning seven of the eight rounds held alongside the World Superbike series. Serafino Foti came second, on another 748 SP. The French tuner Rolando Simonetti, also noted for his association with Raymond Roche's 888cc World Superbikes, prepared Paquay's 748 SP. For this inaugural racing year of the 748 SP, the 750cc twins received a weight advantage over the fours, but, for 1996, this was removed, with all machines needing to weigh in at 172kg. Compared to World Superbike regulations, far fewer modifications were allowed. The engines had to retain the stock camshafts, valve sizes, and airbox shape. Few chassis modifications were allowed either, and the brakes, wheels, and suspension had to be the same as the

production version. In the Italian 600 Supersport Championship Camillo Mariottini won on a factory entry.

For 1996, Simonetti again tuned the Team Alstare 748 SP, now sponsored by the Mexican beer company, Corona. The rider this year was Fabrizio Pirovano, who moved to the Supersport class after a lacklustre year in World Superbike. Again, the 748 SP dominated the series (now called the Open Supersport Championship, as the ten rounds included Japan and Indonesia as well as Europe). Developments to the engine saw the compression rise to 12.4:1 and the power to 115bhp at 11,800rpm. Pirovano won five rounds, Mauro Lucchiari two, and Korner Thoams one, also on 748 SPs.

The Supersport Championship earned world status for 1997, when the Flammini Group launched the Supersport World Cup, a fully televised series run in conjunction with the World Superbike

Fabrizio Pirovano rode the Team Alstare 748 SP to victory in the 1996 Open Supersport Championship. He rode for the team again in 1997 but the machine was unreliable.

After winning the Supersport World Cup in 1997 on the Gio Ca Moto 748 SP, Paolo Casoli has remained the leading Ducati rider in the Supersport Championship. For 2000 he rode the Team Infostrada 748 RS.

Championship. There were eleven rounds for 1997, and, again, the 748 SP won the Championship, though it wasn't as dominant as in previous years as the machine suffered many electrical problems. Despite this, the 32-year-old former Italian champion Paolo Casoli, riding for Gio Ca Moto, took the title. Developments to the 748 SP saw an increase in power to 120bhp at 12,000rpm at the crankshaft. Still only allowed minimal modifications, the Gio Ca Moto 748 SP featured suspension re-worked by Andreani. Casoli won three races and Pirovano one, Pirovano being troubled by mechanical problems on his Team Alstare Corona 748 SP. Although still not a high profile racing class, Ducati's success in the 1997 Supersport World Cup went some way to alleviate its disappointment in Superbike racing. Casoli also won the Italian Supersport Championship in 1997, on the Gio Ca Moto 748 SP.

The success of Daniele Casolari's Gio Ca Moto team during 1997, along with Gio Ca Moto's new association with Ducati Motor, saw the formation of Team Ducati Performance for 1998. Again, Paolo Casoli rode the factory 748, now based on one of the new 748 Racing machines, in the Supersport World Series. With increased emphasis placed on this class by Ducati, factory assistance was also provided to three additional riders: Yves Briguet, Cristiano Migliorati, and Roberto Teneggi. Casoli's machine now produced 117bhp at the rear wheel, and weighed right on the 172kg minimum. Although the 748 Racing was a more serious track machine, the results weren't as good during 1998. Initially complaining that the 1998 bike was slower than his 1997 748, Casoli couldn't repeat his result of the previous year and could only manage fourth overall in the Supersport World Series. He did perform impressively on occasion, winning at Donington and Laguna Seca, yet his consistency let him down. The introduction of the Yamaha R6 was also making life difficult for the 748 Racing which hadn't been developed that much since its inception.

Joining Casoli on a 748 RS, in the Team Infostrada for 2000, was the exciting young Spanish rider, Reuben Xaus.

For 1999, the Supersport World Series became the World Supersport Championship. Team Ducati Performance again entered Paolo Casoli on then 748. However, the raised status of the competition saw an expansion in the number of competitive teams and riders, and the lone 748 was outclassed. Casoli's commitments as Ducati Corse test rider for the factory 996 in the Italian Superbike Championship also saw his performances in World Supersport suffer. Injuries he sustained testing at Rijeka in Yugoslavia, mid-season, meant he missed several rounds, and, without any victories, Casoli finished a lowly 14th overall. Undoubtedly, the 748 Racing was struggling against the continually developed and improved Japanese 600cc fours. This prompted Ducati to offer the 748 R, a homologation special, for 2000.

With the homologation of the 748 R, there was renewed commitment by Ducati in the World Supersport Championship, and for this it produced the most advanced 748 yet: the 748 Racing Special. Two 748 RSs were run alongside the World Superbike machines in the Team Ducati Infostrada. Paolo Casoli again rode the 748, this year being joined by the 22-year-old Spanish rider, Ruben Xaus. Although suppled by Ducati Corse, the 748 RS engines were prepared by Pietro di Gianesin and, at the request of major sponsor Infostrada, the machines were painted red to maintain a similar team profile to that in World Superbike. Immediately, the new 748 RS was more competitive than in 1999, although there were some early problems. Casoli won at Monza and at Brands Hatch, and Xaus at Assen. Casoli finished second in the Championship.

the US also receiving the Biposto for 1998. Also evident this year was a wider variety of models available for specific markets. These included a Monoposto for Japan, and red and yellow Monopostos for California. From November 1998, the Monoposto saddle was also available as an option for all Bipostos, coming with a complete kit that included the taillight and wiring. Another 748, produced only for the US, was a limited edition (102 examples) 748 L. This was painted silver and sold through the prestigious Neiman Marcus mail order catalogue of men's accessories. Essentially, the 748 L was a stock 748 Biposto, but with a carbon-fibre front mudguard and chainguard. The high asking price included a Donna Karan New York leather jacket and Dainese gloves. However, selling motorcycles through a mail order catalogue didn't seem to work as well as the later internet sale of the

Mike Hailwood Evoluzione and 996 R. This was an inspired marketing move that captured the imagination of the buying public with perfect timing.

During 1998, the 748 production of 3491 accounted for nearly 40% of the Hypersport range, and, for 1999, the terminology of the family was changed from Hypersport to Superbike. As the 916 grew into the 996, the 748 received many of the flow-on improvements, and the chassis was virtually identical to that of its larger brother. Unlike the 748 SPS, the 748 received the 520-watt tri-phase alternator that allowed for the high and low beam of the headlights to be run simultaneously. This also overcame the legality issue of the standard headlights in Australia. As with the 996, there were new three-spoke Brembo wheels, these being constructed of GA/Si7, with less silicon than

The 1999 version of the 748 featured new logos, and front forks with a wider brake caliper mount. In other respects, the specification was much as before.

The 748 Racing and 748 Racing Special

To maintain the success of the 748 SP in Supersport racing, a small number (20) of 748 Racing machines were made available to selected teams during 1998. As with the 916 Racing, these were assembled by the racing department. However, with World Supersport regulations limiting the modifications allowed, the 748 Racing wasn't quite as exotic (or as expensive) as the 916 Racing, and retained the single injector IAW 1.6 M CPU and its associated timing layshaft sensor system. Most of the changes incorporated the features of a fully race-kitted 748 SP. Into the engine went a 916 Racing gearbox, sintered clutch plates with stiffer springs, and nimonic valves (in stock sizes of 33mm and 29mm). As the regulations prohibited serious engine modifications, all major components were from the 748 SPS. In the interest of weight saving, there was a lighter clutch cover, a smaller (180-watt) alternator, and shorter, 33mm, carbon-fibre inlet manifolds, these being part of the throttle body after the throttle valve. The throttle bodies were slightly larger than 44mm, which unfortunately did not conform to FIM Supersport regulations. In March 1998, new throttle bodies were suppled to overcome this problem. There was a 916 Racing oil and water cooler and a racing exhaust system with carbon-fibre mufflers. Power was increased slightly over the 748 SP and SPS to 108bhp at 11,500rpm.

More latitude was allowed in chassis modifications, and, here, full racing equipment was specified. This included complete carbon-fibre bodywork (including a sumpguard), carbon-fibre chain guard and mufflers, and a carbon-fibre front dashboard and electronic control unit mount. As there was no lighting, the entire wiring and electrical system was for racing, and there was racing only instrumentation that included a racing rev counter. Along with the revised throttle bodies supplied in March 1998, new FIM Supersport-legal front brake lines were also available. The result of all these modifications took the weight down to 170kg.

For 1999, there was again a limited number (18) of 748 Racing machines produced, these being very similar to that of 1998, but incorporating the revised fairing and tank of the 748 SPS that year. For the 2000 model year, the 748 Racing became the much higher specification 748 RS (Racing Special), using the newly homologated 748 R frame and airbox. Still produced by Ducati Corse, more examples of the 748 RS were initially produced (37). Such was demand that there was soon a second production run of 15. A big development for 2000 was the use of an injection system similar to that of the 996 Factory. Here, a single Marelli IWP 069 injector was placed above the throttle valve, with the throttle body inside the airbox and very short intake ducts. However, Supersport regulations required the injection system to be the same IAW 1.6 M system as the street 748 R, rather than the MF3-S system of the 996 Factory. Regulations allowed for an increase in throttle body diameter to 54mm. There were also a number of engine developments, these including new camshafts (with different timing even to the 748 R), a 12:1 compression ratio, 36mm and 32mm valves, and a racing stainless steel Termignoni exhaust system that consisted of 54 x 0.8mm exhaust pipes. These developments though saw the power increase to 124bhp at 12,000rpm.

Regulations required that the chassis be production based, although the wheelbase was increased 5mm, to 1415mm. Thus, the general chassis (wheels, brakes and front suspension) specifications were as for the 748 R, except for a new generation 'Mark II' Öhlins shock absorber with internal bleeds. The 748 RS also has a different electrical system, with a tri-phase 280-watt alternator.

To maintain the success of the 748 SP – which had won Supersport since 1995 – for 1998, a small number of 748 Racing machines were produced. This is Casoli's Gio Ca Moto machine which he took to fourth place in the 1998 Supersport World Series.

Expanding the 748 line-up for 2000 was a base model, without an adjustable steering head or quick release fairing fasteners. This budget model proved especially popular, and ensured continuity of the 748 range.

before, and saving on rim weight. The Showa front forks also had a wider front brake caliper mount (like the 1998 916 SPS), and there was a completely revised braking system that included a racing-inspired PSC 16mm master cylinder, and braided steel brake lines. Like the 996, the clutch master cylinder, too, was a PSC 13mm, with a stainless steel line and pre-assembled piston. There were also new stainless steel semi-floating 320mm front brake discs with aluminium carriers for the 1999 model year. These discs were slightly thinner than those of the 996, at 4mm. While the 996 received Toshiba front brake pads, the 748 persisted with Ferodo. At the rear, too, was a new Brembo P 32 G brake caliper, and the braking system was an undoubted improvement over that on earlier versions. Completing the small upgrades for 1999 were a new fairing (now with a distinctive '748' logo), fuel tank (now with 'DUCATI'), and revised twin bolt handlebar location. As with the 916, all 748s were recalled, in November 1999, to have

the rear axle checked by a special ultrasonic tester. This included machines from frame number 000001 to 009920.

While 1999 saw demand and production for the new 996 increase considerably over that of the earlier 916, the 748 slumbered. With only 2228 units produced, these accounted for 24% of Superbike production that year. Rather than completely eliminate the smaller line-up, Ducati decided to expand the range to include three models for 2000. Creation of the base 748, in particular, was an inspired marketing move, as was the upgraded specification of the 748 R. Although having a budget model in the range-leading Superbike line-up may have seemed a contradiction, it was highly successful. At a price considerably lower than even the 1999 748 Biposto, the specification of the 748 was barely compromised. Additionally, the 748 engine received all the developments that applied to other 2000 model year machines. These included a new metal head gasket and cylinder assembly, thicker crankshaft shims

A line-up of 748s. This mixture of 748s, 748 Ss, and 748 Rs demonstrates the visual similarity between the three models.

(as on the 996), and bigger crankshaft bearing bushes (also as on the 996). To match these larger bearing bushes were a new pair of timing gears. Other developments included a modified flywheel to accommodate a new bushing on the starter clutch gear and a new oil pressure switch with modified calibration. Completing this new specification were new engine cases with a closed bypass hole. Generally the specifications, though, were unchanged and included the same camshafts, valves, and 31/62 primary drive of before. The 50mm throttle bodies were now shared with the 996 and power was 97bhp at 11,000rpm.

Where the basic 748 differed from the 1999 748 Biposto was in the chassis, and there

reality, few owners bothered to alter the stock steering head angle. Regular 43mm Showa GD 131 forks (with chrome-plated rather than titanium-nitrided fork legs) were fitted, and at the rear was an adjustable Sachs-Boge shock absorber. Also setting the base 748 apart were the bronze-painted, three-spoke Brembo wheels that had been on the 1999 model. The front brakes, too, were improved; the 320mm stainless steel discs now being 5mm thick, with a PSC 16mm master cylinder.

Further budget considerations were apparent in the fairing fasteners, these no longer being the quick release dzus-type, and the flange at bottom of the fuel tank also lacked quick release fittings. However, these features had nothing to do with the functionality of the 748, and it still offered all handling and performance that typified the range. Where it counted, on the road, the 748 was similar to any of its predecessors. Completing the upgraded specification for 2000 was a smaller PS 12mm clutch master cylinder (replacing the PS 13mm), a new sidestand with safety sensor, safety relay, and new wiring. The smaller clutch master cylinder was to improve the hydraulic leverage ratio and reduce muscular effort. Only available as a Biposto, in either red or yellow, the base 748 even weighed slightly less than before, at 196kg dry. It was not surprising that the 748 was immediately popular, allowing the incredible Ducati Superbike experience to an even wider audience.

The middle 748 in the 2000 line-up was the 748 S, this being either red or yellow, and Monoposto or Biposto. Really a development of the 1999 model year 748, the 748 S shared its engine (without an external oil cooler) with the basic 748, but featured a number of chassis improvements. The frame on the 748 S offered the adjustable steering head angle (from 23° 30' to 24° 30' and trail from 91-97mm), and was painted 'gun metal grey,' like the 996

were a number of differences to keep the price down. Most significant was the bronze-painted frame without the eccentric adjustment for steering head and trail, the steering head being set at 24° 30' and the trail at 97mm. This also required a redesigned steering head, and, while it may have appeared to detract from the purity of the original design, in

The middle range 748 for 2000 was the 748 S, available in either Monoposto or Biposto. This shared the Marchesini wheels and gold TiN-coated forks with the 748 R, although the engine specifications were much as before.

Factory racers, to differentiate the S from the base 748. Other features setting it apart from the more basic 748 were Marchesini five-spoke aluminium wheels (also in 'gun metal grey'), these providing 500g less of unsprung weight per wheel. The 43mm Showa GD 131 forks featured gold titanium-nitrided (TiN) fork legs with superior surface hardening and improved sliding. At the rear, the earlier Showa shock absorber was retained. All 748s for 2000 came with new generation Pirelli Dragon Sport EVO radial tyres. Completing the new three-model range was the 748 R, the highest specification machine in the entire 2000 model year line-up (see sidebar). By June 2000, production of the 748, in its various incarnations since 1995, had totalled 17,139.

For the 2001 model year, the same three models of 748 continued, with only detail alterations. The sealed-for-life battery of the 2000 model 996 SPS featured on all models, and there was an improved clutch slave cylinder. All engine mounts were increased

from 10mm to 12mm for greater rigidity and the fourth gear ratio lowered slightly. The highly successful base 748 remained as before, but for the frame and hollow three-spoke Brembo wheels now being painted gun metal grey. Visually, there was now little to separate the 748 from the 748 S, apart from the TiN-coated Showa fork stanchions, Showa shock absorber, and Marchesini wheels.

Although often overshadowed by its larger brothers, by 2001 the 748 had assumed its own individual identity. The 748 in its three incarnations arguably offered the best value of any in the range, the base 748 providing similar looks and handling of the 996 S at considerably less cost. The 748 R on the other hand also provided comparable racing technology to the extraordinary 996 R. Not merely poor relations, these were machines for those who appreciated finesse and balance over outright horsepower.

THE 748 R

Undoubtedly the most exciting new model for the 2000 model year was the 748 R. This offered the highest specification of any production Ducati to date, and was very much a racing machine, with only minimal concessions to make it suitable for road use. Replacing the 748 SPS, in nearly every respect the 748 R provided improved specification. The heart of the 748 R was the homologation of the World Superbike frame and airbox for World Supersport. Previously only available in the British-only 916 SPS Fogarty Replica of 1998, with the 748 R this important development became more widely available.

Apart from the frame and airbox, much development centred on the engine. As featured on the other 2000 748s, this included the metal cylinder head gasket, thicker crankshaft shims, larger crankshaft bushes and new timing gears, and modified flywheel. However, there were many more developments specific to the 748 R. Central to the 748 R engine were new cylinder heads,

without '4V DOHC' lettering and with larger (36mm and 30mm) valves. They also featured the highest lift camshafts ever fitted to a production four-valve Ducati (12.5mm on the inlet and 10.5mm on the exhaust). These camshafts featured revised timing, derived from the 996 Racing, but with closer cam phasing and reduced overlap to reduced exhaust emissions (see Appendix). The valves also had a reduced valve centre distance, so required new valve rockers, and there were slightly stronger valve closing springs. The intake covers were altered to allow for shorter intake manifolds. As with the Ducati Corse 996, the combustion chambers on the 748 R were machined with extremely high precision CNC equipment, though the 748 R retained the normal 748 31/62 primary gears, along with the 748 gearbox. Unlike the 748 SPS, the 748 R had the larger 520-watt tri-phase alternator, this requiring a new crankshaft and alternator cover. The titanium conrods were retained from the 748 SPS.

Other engine developments saw engine cases

Replacing the 748 SPS for 2000 was the even higher specification 748 R. With the revised frame, larger airbox, and a single outboard fuel injector per cylinder this spectacular machine was only available in yellow.

with reversed bolts (like the 996), and the closed bypass hole. The oil pump was now shared with the 996 SPS, having a 25/40 ratio, there also being a new primary drive for the primary drive gear pump. The oil pump featured a built-in bypass and there was a larger diameter bushing for the fixed belt roller. An important improvement was the use of higher quality timing belts (and 19mm wide rather than 17mm), and the racing slipper clutch of the 996 Racing.

The major development was to the frame which now included a much larger capacity airbox (from eight to 14 litres); this incorporating the entire throttle body. There was a single injector located right over the larger (54mm) throttle body, this also being 67mm shorter and combined with shorter intake manifolds and new intake funnels. Developed from the World Superbike MF3-S and Formula One injection system, this used a 'shower form' injection configuration. Along with the specially designed throttle bodies, the new injection system provided improved combustion with effective cylinder filling over a wider rev range. The Weber 1.6 M CPU was retained, although the sensor was Bosch rather

than Marelli. With new Termignoni mufflers, the result of these engine and injection developments saw the production 748 R produce the same 106bhp as the earlier 748 SPS, but at a lower 11,000rpm. The smoother and more progressive torque curve also allowed for an increase in the final drive gearing (with 14- and 36-toothed sprockets). The real benefit of the new engine, however, became evident when it was further developed as the 748 RS for World Supersport racing. In standard form, though, the claimed top speed of the 748 R was around 255km/h, but this was a conservative claim: the Italian magazine *Tuttomoto*, in September 2000, managed 263km/h from its 198kg test machine. The standing start 400m time was 10.9 seconds at 208km/h.

In all other respects, the 748 R was as the 748 S for the 2000 model year. The frame and lighter five-spoke Marchesini wheels were 'gun metal grey,' and the Showa forks featured low friction gold-coloured TiN-coated fork legs. There was the new non-self-retracting sidestand, and the Brembo PSC 12mm clutch master cylinder. The braking system, too, came from 748 S, although with Toshiba TT 2802 sintered front brake pads. Although the front brake discs were no longer the Brembo fully floating cast iron of the 748 SPS, the braking system of the 748 R (with 5mm thick front stainless steel discs) was identical to the 996 (and 996 SPS). With a PSC 16mm master cylinder, it was definitely more than up to the task of stopping the 192kg 748 R. The only feature that was downgraded over the 748 SPS was the rear shock absorber, this being Showa rather than Öhlins. However, this was a small downgrade considering the fantastic racing features incorporated in the engine. As with the 748 SP and SPS, the 748 R was yellow only, and Monoposto, and, of course, it received the new 'Ducati Corse' tachometer. 748 R production was scheduled for 1000 units for the 2000 model year.

As the 748 R was primarily designed for Supersport racing, and given that there were only a small number of 748 RSs available, a Ducati Performance uprating kit was available. Consisting of a complete exhaust system with Termignoni carbon-fibre mufflers, along with a replacement EPROM, this kit immediately gave a 6bhp increase, to 112bhp. Although not eligible for Supersport

In line with the 996 and 748 S, the 748 R received lighter five-spoke Marchesini wheels, painted to match the gun metal grey frame.

For 2001, the 748 R specification was upgraded to include Öhlins suspension and new generation Brembo brakes. The colours were now either yellow or red.

racing in the US, the 748 R was eminently suitable for racing in the AMA Pro Thunder Championship, and proved immediately successful. In the Pro Thunder race at Daytona in March 2000, Shawn Conrad took first place on a 748 R, with Jeff Nash second.

As the 748 R provided Ducati with significantly improved results in the World Superbike Series during 2000, for 2001 there were only moderate developments, all of these intended to enhance racetrack performance. The engine had a lighter flywheel, the lighter crankshaft being balanced with tungsten inserts for improved power response. While the tungsten plugs were heavier than steel, these were designed to offset the more compact sharp profile crank webs to optimum balancing. There was also a lighter piston and titanium valve cotters, all these components intended to provide faster engine acceleration and higher rpm, although power was unchanged. To improve gear selection, there was a vacuum precision-cast desmodromic gear selector drum, this being lighter, as well as providing more accurate gear shifting. Completing the list of upgrades was a carbon-fibre airbox, and the gearbox ratios were now standardised with the 996, with a lower (26/22) fourth gear. All the other ratios were unchanged, although for some strange reason the 748 R (along with the other 748s) still used the 2:1 primary drive.

Now available in either yellow or red (like the Team Infostrada machines), the frame of the 748 R was lighter for 2001, being constructed of 1.5mm thick chrome-molybdenum tubing. The design was similar to that of the 996 R. A major step forward over the 2000 model was the same suspension and brakes as the exclusive range-topping 996 R. These were the racing specification Öhlins 43mm upside down forks with TiN-coated stanchions, along with a racing Öhlins rear shock absorber. The front Brembo braking system was also more racing orientated, the lighter 320mm rotors being thinner (4.5mm instead of 5mm) with fewer floating fasteners (nine) connecting the lightweight ergal carrier to the steel rotors. This saw a reduction in weight of 400g per disc. New racing-inspired calipers featured four 34mm pistons, with four individual pads to provide less wear and resistance on release. There was no doubt that these developments to the already impressive 748 R indicated that Ducati was even more serious in its quest for the World Supersport title during 2001. The higher specification 2001 version also received a numbered plaque on the top triple clamp, although the steering damper was still a Boge unit. With there no longer being a 996 SPS, and the 996 R being in very short supply, the 748 R assumed the position as the highest specification regular production Ducati during 2001.

Sport Touring and Monster four-valve style

After an absence from the Sport Touring market since the demise of the underrated 907 IE in 1992, the ST2 (Sport Touring 2) was unveiled at the Cologne Show, at the end of 1996. This was the first new model to appear following the purchase of Ducati by Texas Pacific Group, but the ST2's origins were really from an earlier era. The design of the ST2 was by Miguel Galluzzi, fresh from his success with the Ducati Monster of 1992, and, as such, the ST2 was very much a Cagiva Ducati. Like Tamburini, Galluzzi stayed with Cagiva after TPG bought Ducati, in 1998. As with many other Ducati designs, the ST2 was ready to go into production some time before its eventual release, but this was delayed due to the company's financial problems of 1995 and 1996.

Unlike the 916, that had been designed from the ground up as a new model over a long period of time, the ST2 drew heavily on existing components and had a much shorter incubation period. Thus, while the frame and suspension may not have been identical to that of current models, the immediacy of production was hastened by using well-tried constituents. The tubular steel frame itself was closely based on that of the Monster,

itself derived from the proven 851/888. With the dual-sided steel swingarm pivoting in the engine crankcases came a monoshock linkage suspension system patterned after the 916. This consisted of a central rod with two ball joints, though the standard set length of 272mm was a little longer than the 261mm of the 916. However, as with the 916, this rod length could be adjusted to provide a different ride height, although this also affected the steering geometry. Also from the 916 came similar forks and brakes, notably superb 43mm Showa forks and the latest specification Brembo braking system. Into this chassis was slotted a developed 907 IE liquid-cooled single overhead camshaft two-valve fuel injected engine, the capacity being increased to 944cc, by boring the 92 x 68mm 904cc engine to 94mm. The engine, though, was more refined, and incorporated the benefits of four years of development. With a Weber Marelli 1.6 M ignition and injection system, 44mm throttle bodies, and a 10.2:1 compression ratio, power was a moderate 83bhp at 8500rpm. This was enough to give the 212kg ST2 adequate performance, especially in the low- and mid-range, and a top speed, without a passenger, of around 225km/h.

Apart from small decals on the tailpiece, the first ST4 of 1999 was virtually indistinguishable from the ST2. Both departed from the earlier 907 IE by not having full coverage bodywork.

On the surface, ST2 specifications may have appeared unremarkable, but the real secret to this motorcycle's excellence was the way it had been designed specifically with sport touring in mind, while retaining the Ducati sporting tradition. It wasn't an easy task to create a touring-style motorcycle over the sporting chassis, but somehow Galluzzi managed to integrate a semi-sporting riding position, provision for a passenger and full luggage within the concept. The result may not have been quite as distinctive as the true sporting Ducatis, but this didn't detract from the machine's excellence. Here was a machine that could cover ground quickly and in comfort, but also provide sporting braking and handling.

Rather than the full coverage fairing of the 907, the ST2 came with European-style full fairing that exposed the engine and tubular steel frame. The fairing was also designed aerodynamically to provide not only improved airflow, but also effective wind protection at high speeds. The ST2 was also the first motorcycle designed with aspheric rear vision mirrors, to give a greater field of vision. Integral in the design were optional colour-coordinated Nonfango bags, and mufflers that could be positioned upwards for more ground clearance, or down when riding with the hard bags. A big departure from earlier sport touring Ducatis was the arrangement of the cockpit; particularly the instruments and handlebars. Unashamedly sporting biased, the instrument panel was derived from that of the 916, dominated by a large tachometer in a polyurethane foam support. In addition to the analogue display

As with all liquid-cooled Ducatis, an unclothed ST4 wasn't particularly pretty. However, the combination of a Desmoquattro 916 engine in an ST2 chassis worked brilliantly.

was a digital panel that provided information such as fuel consumption, fuel reserve, water temperature, and a clock.

The ST2 went into production in April 1997, and it was immediately successful, a total of 4316 being produced that year. Compared with the early production numbers of models in the past, this was considerable. Filling a niche in the marketplace, it was no surprise that the ST2 found itself in the garages of 76% of first-time Ducati buyers. Also, because it drew largely on existing or former models in the line-up, there were very few initial problems. Apart from criticism of the sidestand and gearshift lever, there was little to complain about, and these issues were soon rectified for the 1998 model year.

When the ST2 appeared, it was obvious that this was the first model in a new family, the Sport Touring family, and that, not long afterwards, there would be a four-valve version, the ST4. The ST2 chassis could undoubtedly handle more power, and one of the criticisms

of the ST2 was that, in those markets without strictly enforced speed limits, the 944cc two-valve engine was lacking in top-end power. Also, even with fuel-injection, the two-valve engine was undeniably less refined than the more sophisticated four-valve unit. So it was no surprise when the ST4 was released for the 1999 model year. The only astonishment was that it had taken so long. As far back as January 1998 I was shown several well-used ST4, prototypes in Andrea Forni's development room and told that production had been delayed until July that year. This was due to the imminent release of the Terblanche 900 Supersport.

Creation of the ST4 was a relatively simple operation, given that both the two-valve and four-valve engines shared the same crankcases. However, installing the four-valve 916 engine in an ST2 chassis wasn't quite as straightforward as anticipated. The ST2 was designed with careful attention to weight distribution, and, to maintain this optimum

On the road, the ST4 offered brilliant all-round performance. The aerodynamically designed fairing provided excellent protection, and the motorcycle was easy to ride in all conditions. A gentleman's tourer par excellence.

balance, there had to be some modifications to the 916 engine. Keeping the engine in the same position as on the ST2, and still providing 49% of weight on the front wheel, meant that the front cylinder head needed to be altered slightly, so as to maintain adequate front wheel clearance with the steep (24°) steering head angle. Thus, the exhaust camshaft was moved 10mm closer to the centre of the engine, this already being a successful development from World Superbike racing with new heads homologated for 1998. Other engine developments for the ST4 included a redesigned water pump, and, shared with other 1999 models, an upgraded electrical system that included a new, three-phase, 520-watt alternator instead of the ST2's 420-watt type.

The rest of the engine for the ST4 was basically from the 916 Biposto. There were the same valve sizes of 33mm and 29mm, and camshafts with identical timing and valve lift. With an 11:1 compression ratio, power was 107bhp at 9000rpm. Also from the 916 Biposto were the clutch and six-speed gearbox, although the primary gears were the 32/59 (1.84:1) of the ST2 and 916 SPS. The electronic ignition and injection system was the expected 1.6 M Weber Marelli with single injectors per cylinder. Unlike the 916, with its sealed airbox incorporated within the frame structure, the ST2 had a separate airbox, this also being a feature of the ST4. However, this was redesigned for the ST4, as was the exhaust system and mapping of the CPU, to improve smoothness at lower rpm. The ST4 EPROM was a 072, and there were slightly different versions for the US and Switzerland. Unlike the ST2 (but as with the 916), the ST4 had an external oil cooler, a small black curved radiator mounted underneath the front cylinder.

The result was an engine that really brought the Sport Touring concept to life. Not only did the ST4 perform much more strongly than

the ST2, the engine was smoother and more responsive. It was really only at low rpm that the ST4 suffered in comparison with the ST2, but this was more than compensated for by superior performance in the upper rev range. While the author has enjoyed some time in the saddle of an ST2, when it comes to engine performance nothing matches that of a four-valve Ducati motor on full song. The Ducati four-valve engine is undoubtedly one of the greatest motorcycle engines ever produced, and with the ST4 came a motorcycle that could be ridden all day at high speeds in exceptional comfort. As tested by *Motociclismo* in January 1999, the ST4 was also capable of 244.2km/h, an exceptional speed for a touring motorcycle. The standing start 400m time was 11.190 seconds at 202.6km/h. Here was a sport touring motorcycle more than able to hold its own on the autostrada or autobahn without being intimidated by powerful automobiles. Unlike the ST2, the throttle could be cracked open at 200km/h and the ST4 would leap away.

Housing this spectacular engine was a chassis very similar to that of the ST2. The identical tubular steel frame was constructed in ALS 450, and the steel swingarm pivoted on the rear crankcases, as before. The 55mm diameter steering head tube was located at a fairly steep steering head angle of 24°, giving trail of 102mm. A moderate wheelbase of 1430mm, provided agile, yet stable steering and handling. Complementing this strong chassis was exceptional suspension, this also being identical to that of the ST2. At the front were 43mm Showa GD081 forks providing 130mm of travel, and at the rear was a fully adjustable Showa GD082, the 65mm stroke providing 148mm of rear wheel travel. Another feature of this suspension was the use of large, 25mm diameter axles front and rear, further enhancing rigidity.

Factory-fitted luggage complemented the style of the
ST4, and detracted little from the overall performance.
Fitting the bags required the mufflers to be positioned
lower.

The wheels were three-spoke Brembo, a
3.50 x 17in and 5.50 x 17in, and the braking
system consisted of the usual stainless steel
twin 320mm discs at the front, but with an
888-inspired 245mm disc at the rear. The
front brake calipers were also the usual gold
Brembo P4.30/34 four piston type, but with the
wider caliper mounts of the 1998 916 SPS.

The usual Ferodo Ferit I/D 450 FF brake pads were fitted to the ST4 and the front master cylinder was a Brembo PS 16mm. Surprisingly, although the reservoirs were remotely located

(unlike the ST2), there were no adjustable levers on the ST4. The brake lines were also rubber, contributing to a softness in the braking system. Along with the larger rear disc came a Brembo 34mm twin piston brake caliper and PS 11mm master cylinder. This rear caliper size was increased from 32mm on the 1998 ST2. The tyres, too, came from the ST2, a 120/70 ZR17 on the front, and a considerably smaller tyre on the rear than that of the 916. This was now a 170/60 ZR17. The final drive was by the same DID 525 HV chain, though, because the 916 engine produced its power at higher revs, the final drive ratio was slightly lower than the ST2, with 15- and 43-toothed sprockets.

While ST4 chassis was essentially that of the ST2, there were some other developments for the ST4, these also being shared with the 1999 model year ST2. Although the Brembo three-spoke 17in wheels appeared similar to before, they were constructed of a new alloy with less silicon (GA/Si7). This saw a small reduction in the weight of the wheel rim (400g from the front and 900g from the rear). Though not appearing significant, this reduction in rim weight improved the steering and handling by reducing the gyroscopic effect as well as unsprung weight. Other improvements for 1999 included a new sidestand and gearshift lever. This came from the Monster, and it was now possible to shift gears with large touring-style boots. To overcome fogging of the headlight lens, the headlight design included vented piping. Also new for the ST4 were additional colours: black and dark metallic blue joining red or grey. If any criticism could be levied at the ST4, it was that it was really too similar, visually, and in specification, to the ST2. Apart from small decals on the tailpiece, it was very difficult to tell the two models apart, even though there was a significant price differential. Some of this was rectified for the 2000 model

In addition to the excellent digital display, there was a 'Ducati Corse' tachometer on the ST4 for 2000.

year when the specification of the ST4 was upgraded over that of the ST2.

While the new decals now saw 'ST4' emblazoned in large letters on the fairing, which certainly set the ST4 apart from the ST2, there were also a number of functional improvements. The engine received a metal cylinder head gasket along with a new cylinder assembly, and thicker crankshaft shims along with larger bearing shells (like the 996). There were also new timing gears to match the larger main bearing bushing rings. In line with all 2000 models (including the ST2), there was a modified flywheel to accommodate a new bushing on the starter clutch gear, and a new oil pressure switch with modified calibration. All engine cases for 2000 had a

closed bypass hole. In all other respects, the engine specifications were as before, although the claimed power was reduced to 105bhp at 9000rpm.

There were more developments to the chassis, some being specific to the ST4 rather than the ST2. Both models came with the new sidestand sensor and relay, so that the sidestand no longer automatically retracted, but now incorporated an ignition cut out when down. It had taken many years of complaints, but, finally, this simple problem was efficiently and effectively overcome. Also shared with the ST2 was a power outlet, a standard Kryptonite anti-theft padlock housed in a recess under the seat, and new wiring. The power outlet was designed for electrical accessories, such as electric vests, cellular phones, intercoms, and lights, and had long been a useful feature on other touring machines like the BMW. The socket could also be used to connect a reverse flow battery charger to charge the battery. For 2000, both the ST2 and ST4 received a new 'SPORT TOURING' logo in the fuel tank guard, but lost the rear splash guard. In response to the vulnerability of the fairing paintwork from stone chips, the fairing received a double layer protective transparent coating.

Where the specification between the ST2 and ST4 machines now departed was in the brakes, clutch, and rear tyre. In line with all 2000 models, there were new 320mm stainless steel front discs with aluminium carriers, but on the ST4 these were 5mm thick, rather than the 4mm on the ST2. The ST4 also featured braided steel front and rear brake lines, and the sintered Toshiba TT 2802 front brake pads of the 996. Surprisingly though, there were still no adjustable brake and clutch levers, but, despite this, the braking performance was considerably improved over the 1999 model. The clutch action, too, provided less effort, with a smaller PS 12mm master cylinder

The distinctive matt grey ST4S for 2001: this high
specification sport tourer came with a 117 horsepower
996c engine.

(the ST2 retained the PS 13), and there was
a braided steel clutch line. The final chassis
development for the 2000 model year was an
increase in the size of the rear tyre, to 180/55
ZR17. Further differentiating the two models
was the ST4's Ducati Corse-inspired 'gun metal
grey' frame and wheels. The ST2 retained the
earlier bronze frame and wheels. As before,
there were also colour-matched hard bags
available for the red, yellow, or blue ST4, these
being offered as standard equipment for some
markets. The ST4 also received a revised
dashboard, with an electronic tachometer
with a 'Ducati Corse' logo. The result was a
machine that provided a similar experience

to the first model, but with enough individual
touches to set it apart from the less exciting
ST2.

Further updates to the ST4 appeared for the
2001 model year, including the much-rumoured
996cc version: the ST4S. It was inevitable, as
the 996 S received the 996 SPS engine, that
the base 996 engine would make it into the
ST4. Thus, there were two four-valve sport
touring Ducatis for 2001, the ST4S offering
the highest performance of any motorcycle in
this category. With the ST2 and ST4 virtually
identical to the previous year (except the ST2
also received the 'gun metal grey' frame and
wheels), it was the ST4S that now sported

continued on page 88

The Monster S4

Another project often mooted, over a period of time, was a Monster with a four-valve engine: this finally appearing for the 2001 model year, as the Monster S4. When the Monster first appeared, at the end of 1992, as a 900, it established a niche market for a naked sporting motorcycle, that was continually expanded over the years. So successful was the Monster concept that, by 1999, it comprised 43% of the worldwide Ducati market, although most of these were the basic 600 Dark that was exceptionally popular in Italy. By the year 2000, there was a range of Monsters with two-valve engines from 600 to 900cc, and, for this year, it underwent its first redesign since its inception. Designed initially by Miguel Galluzzi, Pierre Terblanche was responsible for the 2000 updates, which saw a redesigned tail section, front mudguard, and fuel tank. This year also saw the first fuel-injected Monster, the 900 IE, and, following this, it wasn't a huge step to create the four-valve S4. Here, Terblanche used advanced Unigraphics software for the first time to generate computerised 3D-modelling. As a result, the development time was shortened even more that had been evident in Terblanche's earlier projects, such as the 900 Super Sport and Mike Hailwood Evoluzione.

Growing out of the ST4, the Monster S4 shared a similar 916cc engine, but with the same six-speed gearbox as the earlier 996 SPS (and Monster 900 IE). This was identical to that of the 2001 range of Superbikes, except for a slightly higher fourth gear (26/22). Designed primarily as a less hard-edged sporting machine than either the 996/748 Superbike or 900/750 Supersport, the Monster S4 had a re-tuned engine, this featuring the ST4 cylinder heads with a lowered exhaust camshaft. The more compact cylinder heads also enabled the engine to be positioned further forward for optimum weight distribution. There were smaller diameter (40mm) exhaust header pipes, and a larger airbox with a resonator. The stainless steel exhaust pipes came with carbon-fibre heat shields. Most significant, though, was a new, fourth generation, Weber Marelli 5.9 M electronic engine management system, with a 50mm throttle body. A single injector was positioned inside the throttle body. The new Marelli system incorporated CAN logic, and all the components were lighter and more compact than before.

Another important development in adapting the four-valve engine to the naked Monster was to improve the engine aesthetics. Whereas all the other fully-faired four-

An exciting new model for 2001 was the Monster S4. Expanding the best selling Monster range, this took a Desmoquattro 916 engine and placed it in a modified ST4 chassis.

valve engines mounted the battery on the right side of the engine, the S4 featured a light lead-gel maintenance-free battery, this being positioned behind the airbox, above the rear cylinder. This left the front cylinder timing belt cover clearly exposed, and, with the radiator also being cleverly mounted so that it didn't dominate the engine, the right side of the engine looked surprisingly clean for a liquid-cooled design. On the left, it was more of a challenge to make the engine acceptably clean looking. Given that the water pump location was something that couldn't easily be altered, this was done with a new engine cover and pump housing, along with simpler water lines. There was also no external oil cooler. The S4 engine on the left may not have looked quite as neat as the air-cooled 904cc unit, but the benefits of the 916 engine far outweighed those of the less refined air-cooled mill. For a start, the power of the 916 S4 was 101 horsepower at 8750rpm, with 9.3kgm of torque at 7000rpm. Only a full-house Ducati Performance 944 could make that sort of torque and power, and with much less tractability.

In other respects the Monster S4 was very similar to the Monster 900 S. Because the similar racing grey-painted frame was based on that of the ST4, (with 28mm tubes 2mm thick), this provided a 24° steering head angle (rather than 23°), and a slightly longer 1440mm wheelbase. For improved ground clearance, the S4 was 20mm higher, and the swingarm was constructed of aluminium. This featured two rectangular section extruded arms welded to a chill-cast central element. Unlike the Monster 900 S, the wheels were five-spoke Marchesini, still in sizes of 3.50 and 5.50 x 17in, and there was a choice of tyre sizes. The front tyre was either a

120/70 x 17in or 120/65 x 17in, while the rear tyre was a 180/55 x 17in or 190/50 x 17in. At the front, there were the same 43mm Showa upside down forks, and, in line with other 2001 models, the S4 received a Sachs shock absorber. This Sachs unit featured a piggyback reservoir. The brakes were from the ST4, with twin front 320 x 5mm discs, P4 30-34mm calipers, and a PSC 16mm master cylinder. Also from the ST4 was the rear 245mm disc and Brembo two-piston brake caliper. Other developments shared throughout the entire range for 2001 included 12mm engine mounts.

The styling of the Monster S4 was an evolution of the Terblanche Monster restyle for the 2000 model year. There was a new dashboard, now incorporating a water temperature warning light, and an electronic immobiliser with transponder. Carbon-fibre was used for the small front fairing, mudguards, side body panels and timing belt covers. The two-piece handlebars also mounted directly on the top triple clamp, as with the ST4. With a weight (including battery, oil and coolant) of 193kg, the Monster S4 was only 2kg up on the two-valve 900 S, yet provided considerably enhanced performance. Colours for the 2001 model year were red, silver, black, chrome, and 'gun-metal grey' with red wheels. With the Monster S4 offering the legendary 916 engine in a lightweight chassis with a more upright riding position, undoubtedly Ducati had another winner on its hands. Also, given the attention paid to obtain optimum weight distribution, the Monster S4 may prove to be one of the finest performing and best handling naked motorcycles available, in what has become an increasingly competitive sector in the marketplace.

As a top-of-the-range model, the Monster S4 was adorned with carbon-fibre. The general engine layout was also tidier than on full-faired versions.

more high quality performance components. The only engine developments to the ST4 were the larger (12mm) engine mounts, and new oil pipe lines to the oil cooler, with double O-rings for improved sealing at high pressures. The chassis included Sachs adjustable shock absorber and thinner (4mm) front brake discs.

Most development was saved for the range-leading ST4S. Even back in 1998, Ducati's then-CEO, Federico Minoli, had hinted that the ST2 might soon receive the 996 SPS engine, to create the ultimate sport tourer: the ST4S that emerged for 2001 didn't actually get the high-performance SPS engine, but the 996 unit was retuned to produce slightly more power.

As with the ST4, the exhaust camshaft was lowered, but the general engine specifications were as for the 996. This included the 36mm and 30mm valves and identical camshafts. Where the ST4S departed was in the gearbox and injection system. Whereas the entire range of 748 and 996 Superbikes received a closer ratio gearbox for 2001, the ST4S (and ST4) retained the earlier 996 gearbox. The injection system was the fourth generation Weber 5.9 M, this being similar to that of the Monster S4, but with twin simultaneous injectors, as with the 996. The CPU also incorporated an immobiliser function, and there was a new fuel pump with a lighter, more compact flange. With 117bhp at 8750rpm, and 10kgm of torque at 7000rpm, the ST4S promised exceptional performance and a top speed in excess of 250km/h.

Although the chassis of the ST4S was similar to that of the ST4, there were some important developments. Along with the 12mm engine mounts shared throughout the range, the swingarm was aluminium rather than steel. Other developments saw TiN-coated Showa forks, an Öhlins rear shock absorber, and five-spoke Marchesini wheels. The wheels saved 1kg, and came shod with high-performance Michelin Pilot or Pirelli Dragon Evo tyres, these

the same size as the ST4. The Öhlins shock absorber featured a spring pre-load remote control that could be adjusted while on the move. Completing the high specification of the

Completing the ST4S's upgraded specification over
the ST4 were Marchesini wheels and improved brakes.

ST4S was new Asahi-Denso switchgear, and
carbon-fibre mudguards. Colours included matt
grey, in addition to the regular red, black or
yellow. Again, Ducati had pursued the path of
evolution through the marriage of other families
with the ST4S. With a more powerful engine
than the 996, the ST4S took this to a new level.

The 996 replaced the 916 for 1999, but there was more to the new model than simply a larger engine, and the 996 retained the mantle as bench mark sporting twin.

The 996

The release of the Honda VTR1000F, Suzuki TL1000S, and Aprilia RSV Mille – all 1000cc V-twins – prompted Ducati to increase the displacement of the 916 Biposto to a full litre. Thus the 1999 model year saw the birth of the 996, replacing the 916 Biposto. As the 916 SPS had been 996cc since 1997, this was a relatively simple process, yet there was more to the new model than just a larger engine: again, Ducati managed to maintain its lead as bench mark sporting twin with the 996.

For 1999, the family terminology was changed from Hypersport to Superbike, and, with this, came the first major revisions to the 916 since its inception in 1993. Most of these developments were to the engine, now based on that of the 916 SPS of 1997 and 1998. This featured the stronger crankcases with a wider cylinder stud pattern to comfortably allow for 98mm pistons with a respectably thick cylinder liner. However, there was more to the engine than simply larger pistons, and the entire intake and exhaust tuning was redesigned. This saw not only the maximum power and torque increase, but also the general power characteristics improve, which improved overall rideability. Once again, Ducati engineers had shown that there was considerable life left in the venerable four-valve desmodromic engine design.

Although the 996 engine was ostensibly developed from the 1998 916 SPS, it still incorporated many features of the 916 Biposto.

From the SPS came the crankcases, 11.5:1 98mm pistons and the cylinder heads with the wider stud layout and larger valves (36mm inlet and 30mm exhaust). For extra strength, the crankcases had reversed bolts. The primary drive ratio was also that of the SPS (32/59), but in most other respects the specification was that of the 916 Biposto. This included the 916 desmodromic camshafts (with mild timing and relatively low lift) and gearbox, but with a new crankshaft (of higher tensile strength to handle the increased power), and a revised clutch basket and clutch actuation system. With the stronger crankshaft came larger crankshaft bearing shells and thicker crankshaft shims. The conrods were still the forged steel 916 Biposto type, but driven on. Also from the 916 Biposto was the 1.6 M Weber injection system with only one engine sensor, but this was revised to incorporate twin injectors per cylinder and known as the 1.6 M.B1. As the 1.6 M was primarily a single point injection system, the CPU, which also had a new 074 EPROM, triggered both the injectors simultaneously. As with the 916, the US and Switzerland received an EPROM with slightly different mapping. The 1.6 M.B1 was unlike the P8 system of the 916 and 996 SPS which triggered the two injectors sequentially. Complementing the revised injection system was a new airbox with improved sealing, shorter venturi-shaped intake ducts, and larger volume mufflers to further reduce noise

continued on page 95

The 996 SPS

As a highly successful concept to promote the entire range, the 996 SPS was upgraded for the 1999 model year to further elevate it above the regular 996. While the general engine specifications remained unchanged from the 1998 916 SPS, new for 1999 was the 520-watt tri-phase alternator. This also allowed for the 996 SPS to be legal in Australia with the standard headlight set-up. As with the 996, this meant a new crankshaft, though the 996 SPS retained the forged titanium conrods. There was also a new oil pump for the 996 SPS, with a 25/40 ratio. This required a different primary drive gear, and a different oil delivery pipe to the cylinder heads. With the upgrading of the 996 to 112bhp, along with brake and suspension improvements, the gap between it and the SPS narrowed. So, while retaining the Öhlins rear shock absorber and steering damper, but to elevate its status above the 996, for 1999 the 996 SPS received five-spoke Marchesini wheels. These were patterned

after those on the World Superbike racers, but still manufactured by Brembo. The Marchesini wheels had first appeared on the limited production Fogarty Replica 916 SPS of 1998 and were even lighter than the new type of three-spoke Brembo (by around 500g per wheel). They retained the same sizes of 3.50 x 17in and 5.50 x 17in. The front braking system, though, was identical to that of the 996, with the 320 x 5mm stainless steel discs replacing the earlier fully floating cast iron type. The 996 SPS still came with a small silver plaque on the top triple clamp, but production was considerably less than in 1998, with only 658 manufactured. These were all red. A second edition of the 996 SPS was also produced, later in 1999. Known as the 996 SPS 2, it was identical but for different cylinder heads, manufactured in a different alloy for homologation requirements. Only 150 of this second series of 996 SPS was produced, all in European specification. With the

Now officially a 996 SPS, for 1999 the range leader received Marchesini five-spoke alloy wheels.

Another series of Fogarty replicas was produced for 1999, this time being available outside Britain and numbering 150. As before, Ducati Performance racing decals distinguished them.

success of the small number of 916 SPS Fogarty Replicas produced during 1998 only for Britain, 150 1999 specification 996 SPS Factory Replicas were produced, this time for Europe, Japan, and Australia. These also came complete with decals patterned on the Ducati Performance racing 996, and a special numbered plaque for that series. They also had the 43mm Showa forks with gold-coloured, low friction, titanium nitride (TiN) fork legs, that would feature on all 2000 model year 996s.

There was the inevitable upgrading of the specification of the 996 SPS for the 2000 model year. The engine was unchanged but for a modified flywheel, to accommodate a new bushing on the starter clutch gear, and a new oil pressure switch with revised calibration. The Weber electronic injection system was still the now-ancient P8 – the 2000 series 996 SPS would be the final Ducati to feature this venerable, but effective, system. Further engine upgrades would wait until the new short-stroke 998 for 2001, so it was the chassis that received more attention, continuing a successful system of planned obsolescence. This may have just been shrewd marketing to maintain the status of the 996 SPS, but it was undoubtedly profitable. Unlike Ducatis of the past, where the first model in

Annual upgrading of the 996 SPS specification saw Öhlins forks for the 2000 model year. Otherwise, there were few changes.

the series was often the best and most desirable, with Ducatis of the TPG era this was no longer the case. Not only was the 2000 model year 996 SPS the finest example yet of its genre, it arguably offered the best sporting performance available.

Although the new non-retracting sidestand, PS 12mm clutch master cylinder, new wiring, and 'Ducati Corse' tachometer were also shared with the 996, new for 2000 were 43mm Öhlins front forks, a lighter aluminium rear subframe, and maintenance-free battery with new mount. This 'sealed-for-life' battery saved 1.1kg in weight. The frame and wheels were also 'gun metal grey' this year, and the total weight 3kg less than before, at 187kg dry.

The Öhlins forks also came with gold-coloured TiN coated fork legs, but featured some developments from the World Superbike racing programme. The 85mm steering lugs were from the Ducati Corse 996, and, along with new, stiffer, triple clamps, the axle mounting height was

reduced from 110mm to 80mm. This had also featured on the Ducati Corse 996, and allowed for an increase in the extension of the stanchions, to provide more precise front end control. The rear subframe was now constructed of aluminium tubing, using the same cross-section as the Ducati Corse 996, and saving 0.5kg. These developments maintained the position of the 996 SPS as the world's premier sports bike. It may not have been the fastest Superbike, but the suspension improvements elevated the 996 SPS beyond that of even the newer generation Japanese and Italian machines. It was a true case of racing improving the breed, something that wasn't really evident in the competition until the advent of the Honda RC 51. It was really only the absolute excellence of the 996 SPS and the 996 Factory racer that prompted Honda to produce the RC 51, and discontinue development of the four-cylinder RC 45. Even the much-lauded MV 750 F4, the next generation Tamburini design, had yet to prove itself on the track.

Following requests for more examples of the Factory Replica 996 SPS, another series was produced for 2000. Originally, this was to be known as the 996 SPS 3, but it was officially known as the 996 Factory Replica 2, and was primarily for the homologation of new parts for the 996 Factory 2000 World Superbike racer. 147 of these 996 Factory Replica 2 were produced in the first production run.

As with all the 996s for 2000, the 996 SPS's Öhlins forks featured gold-coloured, TiN-coated fork stanchions.

levels. These were now 120 x 420mm, still with the restrictive 45mm exhaust. A noticeable difference between the 996 and its predecessor was the oval-section exhaust header pipes. Along with the ST4 and 748 (but not the 748 SPS) came a new 520-watt tri-phase alternator and alternator cover. This more powerful alternator was primarily designed to allow for a more powerful headlamp, and one capable of running high and low beams simultaneously, so that on low beam both headlights were operating. One of the primary reasons for this development was to circumvent the peculiar law in Australia that outlawed the earlier 916-style headlight. While the new alternator was an improvement electrically, there were still problems with loosening on the crankshaft, and it was important that the alternator tightening was checked at the first service.

These developments resulted in an engine that produced 112bhp at 8500rpm. This was considerably less than the peakier 916 SPS, and the emphasis was more on mid-range power. While still out-gunned by Suzuki and Aprilia in the top end, the 996 more than made up for it in the chassis, which remained unequalled, especially on the racetrack. This chassis was largely unchanged from the 916, but received some important developments. Although there was a new fairing and fuel tank (and new decals), most of the changes were to the front brakes and suspension. From the 1998 916 SPS came the Showa front forks with revised sliders, to allow for the fitting of the new type wider mount Brembo brake calipers. Not only did the wider mounts claim to increase rigidity, there was different internal plumbing. Along with these new calipers were sintered (rather than organic) Toshiba TT 2802 brake pads, and a PSC 16mm front master cylinder derived from the Brembo racing radial type. The clutch master cylinder, too, was of this new generation, this being a PSC 13mm. Finally,

the thin warp-prone stainless steel discs of the 916 made way for new 320mm semi-floating stainless steel discs, now 5mm thick. These also had flanges with steel studs. Combined with stainless steel brake lines, the braking system was finally up to the standard of the rest of the machine. Completing this improved specification was a stainless steel clutch line, pre-assembled with the piston to ensure air-free operation. The rear braking system, too, was upgraded with a stainless steel brake line, along with a new Brembo P 32 G brake caliper, still with Ferodo Ferit I/D 450 FF brake pads.

In line with other 1999 models, the 996 received new, lighter 3.50 x 17in and 5.50 x 17in wheels constructed of GA/Si7 with a lower silicon content. There was a small change to the handlebar mounts (with two bolts) and a revised seat mount. The resulting 996 not only produced more power than the 916, it also weighed slightly less, at a claimed 198kg dry. As with the previous 916, the 996 was available in red or yellow, and generally only Biposto. In the US, the 996 was also available as a Biposto or Monoposto, the Monoposto 996 also being available in Japan. With the 996 SPS not street-legal in the US, there was an additional variant offered, the 996 S (Special). The 996 S was specifically for California, and mated the Monoposto 996 SPS chassis with five-spoke Marchesini wheels and Öhlins rear shock absorber and steering damper with the standard street-legal 996 engine. Also from the 996 SPS came an assortment of carbon-fibre body parts, and a special numbered plaque on the top triple clamp, but not the aluminium rear subframe. Also unlike the 996 SPS, the 996 S was available in yellow, and 200 red and 200 yellow were manufactured for the 1999 model year.

By 1999, the quality problems that saw the number of recalls during 1998 seemed to have been resolved. However, following a

New for the 2000 996 were Marchesini wheels, TiN-coated forks, and new brake rotors. The 2001 model shown here was virtually identical.

fatal accident in Germany attributed to rear axle failure on a 916, there was a safety recall for the 996 in November 1999. This included machines from chassis number 000001 to 001311, and required the rear axle to be ultrasonically tested for defects. As for performance, the 996 delivered exactly what it set out to do, this being mid-way between the 916 and 916 SPS. As tested by *Cycle's Sportbike 2000,* the 996 produced 106 rear wheel horsepower at 8600rpm. The measured top speed was 161mph (259km/h) and the quarter-mile acceleration was 10.93 seconds at 129.5mph (208.4km/h). These figures placed the 996 almost on a par with the Aprilia RSV Mille.

For the 2000 model year, there were only detail improvements to the 996. The engine received a modified flywheel to accommodate the new bushing on the starter clutch gear, and there were new oil pipes to cylinder heads (from the 996 SPS). The only other engine modification was to the oil pressure switch, this featuring revised calibration. What really set the 2000 996 apart were the new five-spoke Marchesini wheels (painted 'gun metal grey' like the frame), and Showa forks with gold TiN (titanium-nitrided) fork legs. As with other Superbikes for 2000, there was the PS 12mm clutch master cylinder, new wiring, 'Ducati Corse' tachometer, and sidestand with a safety sensor, so that the machine couldn't be started with the sidestand down. As before, the 996 was available in either Biposto or Monoposto, and in red or yellow. All 996s received Michelin Pilot radial tyres.

Again, for the US, there was a 996 S, this still being a standard 996 engine in a 996 SPS-derived chassis. Thus, the Monoposto 996 S had an Öhlins shock absorber, and an aluminium rear subframe, but retained the 43mm Showa forks of the 996. For 2000, the 996 S was red only, and, by June

2000, Ducati had produced 26,613 units of the 916/996 in its various versions.

For the 2001 model year, the 996 range was expanded to include three models, with the previous 996 SPS engine powering the new 996 S. There were only small changes to the 996, the main one being to include an Öhlins rear suspension unit. While the engine was identical to that of the previous year, a closer ratio gearbox was standardised throughout the Superbike range. All the ratios were as with the earlier 996 SPS but for a slightly lower (26/20 instead of 26/22) fourth gear. The 996 also received a sealed-for-life battery and new Brembo clutch slave cylinder.

Because the 996 R superseded the previous 996 SPS, a new model was created for 2001: the 996 S. This slotted in-between the exotic limited production 996 R and regular 996. It took the magnificent 123bhp 996 SPS engine, and placed it in either a Monoposto or Biposto 996 chassis. However, while the essential engine specifications were that of the 996 SPS, the P8 injection system was changed to the 1.6 M with the twin simultaneous injectors of the 996. These were also positioned inside the 50mm throttles.

In a world where the advance of computer technology is dramatic, it is quite amazing that the P8 processor lasted on the top-of-the-line Ducati from 1993 until 2000. With the 1.6 M injection system came a single Bosch engine sensor, although the other components (including titanium conrods) were the same as for the 996 SPS. One benefit from the 1.6 M CPU (and sealed battery) was a saving in weight of around 2kg. Also new for the 996 S was the slightly lower fourth gear, the gearbox being shared throughout the Superbike range.

To widen the appeal of the 996 S, the frame was that of the regular 996, with a steel, rather than aluminium, rear subframe designed to accommodate a passenger on the Biposto

continued on page 100

The 'Testastretta' (Narrow-Head)

For a design that owed its origins to Fabio Taglioni's 500cc Pantah of 1976, the success of the 996 right through until the turn of the century was astounding. There were repeated calls in the press for a new engine, but the success of Ducati's process of continual refinement and evolution was difficult to argue with. Even by 2000, the 996 engine was responding to consistent development, but Massimo Bordi knew that his Desmoquattro, already over ten years old, couldn't last forever. During 1999, three examples of the new 998 were produced, and, early in 2000, Luca Cadalora tested the Testastretta on the track. Over the years, there had been many rumours of a completely new engine, with a narrower cylinder angle and possibly an alternative valve operating system. There were also indications of a new chassis to replace the 916, but the reality was that Ducati didn't have the resources to produce either an all-new engine, or complete motorcycle, in a short space of time. In international terms, Ducati was still a small company. Even the 916 had taken six years to develop, and the engine design was carried over from an existing model. The absolute success of the 916/996 was such that it would be extremely difficult to replace, and there was much discussion amongst the directors of the company as to the form this should take.

The new Testastretta engine featured narrower cylinder heads, a deeper sump, and fuel injectors mounted above the intakes.

However, in the face of the new twin cylinder competition, specifically the Honda RC 51 and Aprilia RSV Mille, it is inevitable that the Ducati engine would need to be revised. Aprilia already had a shorter stroke RSV Mille SP (100 x 63.4mm) homologated for World Superbike, and the Honda RC 51 had similar dimensions at 100 x 63.6mm. So, while some may have been surprised that the 998 was only another evolution of the four-valve engine, this was only to be expected. With a completely new-generation engine possibly up to ten years away, the 998 needed to provide the scope for another series of evolutionary steps, and the ability for Ducati to remain at the forefront of World Superbike. Central to this was the search for higher revs, and improved cylinder filling and combustion. The higher revs came from a shorter stroke (63.5mm), the stroke being similar to that of the older 888, and allowing revs to climb to 13,000rpm. This stroke, combined with a larger bore (100mm), provided 998cc. More important was a new cylinder head design, with revised rocker positioning to provide for a narrower (25°) included valve angle. Apart from making the cylinder head more compact, the primary goal with the new head was to reduce the included valve angle so as to maintain a high compression ratio with excellent combustion. The previous included valve angle of 40° was inherited from the Cosworth DFV of 1968, and was a limiting factor in achieving the high compression ratios that were required, and allowed for, by the more advanced fuels of the end of the 1990s. Always a problem with Ducati engines that were a product of evolutionary development, wide included angles meant that, to achieve a high compression ratio, the pistons needed a high dome. This was less than optimum for perfect combustion; the problem had occurred as far back as 1972, with the 750 Desmo and its wide 80° included valve angle. In those days, twin sparkplug ignition alleviated the combustion problem, and, on the 996, sophisticated electronic engine management allowed for continuous development of the four-valve Ducati engine.

The design of the new, more compact, cylinder head commenced in early 1998 with the assistance of an outside consultant, Ing Marchetti. Using outside consultants in engine development wasn't new to Ducati: in the past, it had approached Armaroli and Ricardo. Marchetti came with over 30 years experience with Ferrari Formula 1 engineering, and had an association with HPE (High-performance Engineering), a company jointly owned by Ducati and Piero Ferrari. He worked in collaboration with Ing Massimo Bordi, but unfortunately died during 1999 without seeing the project completed.

With the existing Desmoquattro valve rocker system, all four rockers were positioned inside the valves and this arrangement did not lend itself to the design of a compact cylinder head. Bordi's original four-valve desmodromic thesis of 1975 had the rockers located outside the valves, but the outboard position of the closing rocker compromised the port angle. Bordi and Marchetti's solution was to combine the two systems, with the opening rocker arms positioned outwards, while the closing rockers were kept inside. The difficulty came with the support of the closing arms inside the head while maintaining a central sparkplug. Marchetti's solution was to insert a steel sleeve down the centre of the sparkplug insert. With this problem solved, development of the engine proceeded quickly. After many years of having the camshafts turning in ball bearings, the camshafts now ran directly in the cylinder head, these located with caps. This system had long been used by Japanese manufacturers, and was done to simplify camshaft removal and reduce noise. Another benefit was a more compact cylinder head, with the possibility of future installation in a shorter chassis with the engine closer to the front wheel. With the intake valves inclined 12°, and the exhaust valves 13°, the shallower combustion chamber allowed for a compression ratio of 11.4:1 with a flat-topped piston. The larger bore also allowed for an increase in intake valve diameter to 40mm, and the exhaust valve to 33mm.

It wasn't only the heads that were new on the Testastretta. While retaining the same vertically split arrangement as before, the crankcases were redesigned to reduce weight and improve lubrication, and were generally strengthened to cope with the projected power increase in World Superbike form. The sump featured a deeper configuration, this designed primarily for racing so the oil pressure would remain consistent during extreme acceleration or deceleration, when the oil level could get low. Also new for the Testastretta was a new-generation 5.9 M Marelli electronic ignition and injection control unit. The ignition coils were a stick-type that sat directly on top of the sparkplug. As with the 2000 model 748 R, this featured a single central 'raindrop-style' injector and a 54mm throttle body, although the injectors were neatly mounted in plastic retainers over the throttle bodies. The resulting engine, as fitted to the production 996 R (with oval aluminium mufflers), provided 135 horsepower at 10,200rpm (10% more than the 996 SPS), with a maximum torque of 10.3kgm at 8000rpm. Although, for 2001, the new engine was placed in a similar chassis to the previous 996 SPS, the more compact engine was undoubtedly designed with a new frame in mind at some future date. According to Massimo Bordi, this was to be Ducati's spearhead for the next decade, "We don't release new engines very often," he told the author, "and, when we do, they need to provide a basis for constant evolution over a long time."

Unlike the Desmoquattro, the Testastretta opening valve rockers were positioned outside the camshafts, enabling the camshafts to be closer together.

As the next generation of four-valve Ducati engine, the Testastretta also featured a narrower included valve angle.

For 2001, the base 996 included an Öhlins rear shock absorber and a revised Brembo clutch slave cylinder.

version. The suspension, too, was that of the 996 rather than the 996 SPS, with TiN-coated Showa forks and an Öhlins rear suspension unit. The Öhlins steering damper made way for a Boge, and, unlike the SPS, which had always been red, the 996 S was also available in yellow.

Even as Ducati entered the first decade of the new millennium, the 996 still represented the pinnacle of sporting motorcycle design. For a design nearly a decade old, the style has remained ageless and resilient to the whims of fashion in the increasingly fickle world of motorcycle style. However, just as the 888 reached its limit as a pure racing design, the same has inevitably happened to the 996. The rate of technological progress may have

slowed during the 1990s, but, by 2000, the 996 wasn't anywhere near as dominant on the racetrack as it had been only a year earlier. The Testastretta engine gave the 996 a new lease of life, but, by 2002, a replacement for the 996 was already expected. Its eventual form was the subject of much discussion at Borgo Panigale, and speculation in the motorcycle press. Ducati's designer, Pierre Terblanche, was fully aware of the difficulties faced in creating a new Superbike, knowing he had to take the legendary 996 design to another dimension. While Ducatisti the world over awaited his creation with apprehension ultimately history was unkind to the 916/996 successor, the 999.

The 996 R

The first production motorcycle to feature the new Testastretta engine was the range-leading 996 R, replacing the 996 SPS for 2001. Built as a limited production of 500 units, 350 were sold immediately over the internet on the release of the model on September 12, 2000. Again this showed the brilliance of Ducati's marketing department, as visually the 996 R looked little different from its predecessor. As with earlier SPs and SPSs, the 996 R kept the earlier model designation, even though the engine displacement was 998cc. This was an historical precedent that began with the 851 SP2 and SP3 of 1990-91, and had continued with the 916 SPS of 1997-98. Intentionally done to retain links with the earlier design and maintain family uniformity, there would eventually be a designated 998 to replace the 996 R. In the meantime, though, the 996 R epitomised eight years of development of the 916, and showed the world that this great motorcycle was not to be dismissed lightly.

Apart from the new brakes, the 996 R may have looked outwardly similar to the 996 SPS, but under the fairing lurked the new generation Testastretta desmodromic engine.

There wasn't only a new engine for the 996 R; the chassis and bodywork, too, were revised. The red-painted fairing was constructed of carbon-fibre, and was without the side vents of other 996s. This was claimed to reduce drag by 0.02 Cx points. The frame was a modified Fogarty-type, constructed of 2mm chrome-molybdenum tubing, with an aluminium rear subframe. As with all 2001 models, the engine mounting bolts were increased to 12mm.

Braking upgrades for the 996 R included thinner (4.5mm instead of 5mm) 320mm front discs, with nine ergal floating fasteners connecting the lightweight ergal disc carrier to the steel rotor. These discs were 400g lighter than before, and were gripped by new four-pad Brembo calipers with four 34mm pistons. These were similar in design to those used on the World Superbike racers and provided less friction on release, as well as more uniform pad wear. Completing the specification were the usual Öhlins 43mm forks, shock absorber, and steering damper. With 135bhp on tap, the 996 R would undoubtedly raise the ante and set the new performance standard for two-cylinder sports bikes. However, being a very expensive limited edition only, most seemed destined for collections, and it was unlikely that many made it onto the street.

The 996 R carbon-fibre fairing no longer included side vents, and was claimed to be more aerodynamic than before.

Superbike Champion

As with all great Ducatis, the 916 was created primarily as a racer, then adapted for the street. Thus, while it may have been a compromised road motorcycle, particularly with regard to comfort, as a racing machine the 916 has proven competitive year after year. And, as had been evident in the past with Ducati, the secret to the 916's success has been constant evolution of the concept. Whereas other companies may introduce a completely new design every few years, slowing the development process, Ducati has resisted this, and maintained a commitment to evolution, not revolution.

Also not to be discounted is the 'Fogarty factor.' While other riders have also had success on the Bolognese bikes, Carl Fogarty's riding style seemed particularly suited to the 916's power and handling characteristics. Arguably, Fogarty may be the greatest rider ever in the history of Superbike World Championship, but the combination of Fogarty and the Ducati 916/996 has proved without equal.

One of the most significant advantages of the 916 over the earlier 888 was the compactness of the design, and small overall size. More similar to a pure Grand Prix machine in dimensions (if not weight), the 916 made the lighter 888 seem tall, wide, and fat. For a new model, the 916 was also surprisingly successful – despite some initial handling and setting-up problems. After a slow

Although it went down to the final round, Fogarty clinched the 1994 World Superbike Championship in the 916's inaugural year.

A study in concentration and psychological dominance:
the great British rider Carl Fogarty has played an
integral part in the success of the 916/996 in World
Superbike, and, between 1994 and 2000, the names
Fogarty and Ducati were synonymous with victory.

Fogarty in action during 1994: this was the final year for carbon brakes, these with shrouds to maintain higher temperatures.

start in its inaugural racing season of 1994, with development hampered after Fogarty broke his wrist at Hockenheim in May, Fogarty came back to win the 1994 World Superbike Championship. Although it went down to the final race at Phillip Island, the result was especially pleasing for both Fogarty and Ducati. They had only narrowly missed out on the 1993 Championship on the well-developed 888, though Ducati still retained the constructor's title that year.

1994

For 1994, Virginio Ferrarí replaced Raymond Roche as team manager of the official factory Ducati racing team. Ferrari, a former world class racer who had finished second in the 1979 500cc World Championship, also had a long association with Cagiva and Ducati. In 1985, he won the Italian Formula One Championship on a factory 750 F1, and had ridden the prototype 748 in 1986. In the Virginio

Ferrari team, alongside Fogarty, was Giancarlo Falappa. However, this was to be Falappa's final season, as he sustained serious injuries following a crash whilst testing at Albacete, in Spain, in June.

After suffering from a hefty weight penalty since the inception of the World Superbike Championship, for the 1994 season the 750cc four-cylinder bikes received a weight reduction of 5kg, to 160kg. This narrowed the gap between the fours and the twins to only 15kg, and, to maintain the 916 Racing's competitiveness, the longer stroke 916 engine was bored 2mm to create 955cc. Following many years of using relatively small valves to produce a wide and strong mid-range without severely compromising top end, the 955cc engine now had 37mm inlet and 31mm exhaust valves. There were also titanium Pankl conrods (with 21mm gudgeons), and forged British Omega 11.6:1 pistons. Titanium valves were tried, but were the cause of several engine failures throughout the season. Other engine problems were due to valve rocker failure

James Whitham rode one of the few 916 Racing machines available for 1994. Sponsored by the British distributor Moto Cinelli, he won a World Superbike round in Indonesia.

caused by new camshafts with extremely steep opening and closing ramps. These new camshafts were developed at Bologna by a team headed by Luigi Mengoli and Franco Farnè. Although they had long duration, the valve lift was moderate, with 11mm of inlet valve lift and 10.5mm of exhaust valve lift. The inlet valve opened 31° before top dead centre, closing 78° after bottom dead centre, and the exhaust valve opened 71° before bottom dead centre, closing 45° after top dead centre. Running 102 octane AGIP fuel, the 955 produced 150bhp at 11,000rpm at the gearbox, and was safe to 12,000rpm. A German KLS electronic gearshift was also used this year, allowing for ⅒ of a second shifting.

Chassis developments over the street 916 included 46mm Öhlins forks, and an Öhlins rear suspension unit, but, in racing form, the 916 chassis exhibited some deficiencies. Following a Mugello test session mid-season,

Massimo Tamburini made some changes to the chassis. "We needed to get some more weight on the front wheel and improve the traction at the back," Tamburini said, "so we lengthened the swingarm 20mm." The magnesium swingarm also weighed 1kg less, helping to push the weight bias forward. "The swingarm included a 50mm axle (up from the standard 35mm), and we made the rear hub and eccentric adjuster larger. That allowed the rear wheel to be moved back further, increasing the wheelbase another 8mm, to 1428mm." Further developments led to a revised lever for the rear suspension, raising of the ride height, and the setting of the steering head angle to 24.5°, giving 100mm of trail, to create stability. To get even more weight on the front wheel the front axle was solid. These changes saw the 916 finally handle well as a racer.

In an endeavour to attain the class minimum of 145kg, fairly advanced weight

World Superbike Championship victories 1994

World Superbike Champion; Carl Fogarty (Ducati 916)
World Superbike Constructor's Championship; Ducati 916

2 May	Donington Park, GB	Race 1	Carl Fogarty
29 May	Misano, Italy	Race 2	Giancarlo Falappa
19 June	Albacete, Spain	Race 1 & 2	Carl Fogarty
17 July	Zeltweg, Austria	Race 1 & 2	Carl Fogarty
21 August	Sentul, Indonesia	Race 1	James Whitham
		Race 2	Carl Fogarty
11 September	Assen, Holland	Race 1 & 2	Carl Fogarty
25 September	Mugello, Rep. San Marino	Race 2	Carl Fogarty
30 October	Phillip Island, Australia	Race 1	Carl Fogarty

saving measures were adopted. There were magnesium engine covers, and all the bodywork was in carbon-fibre, with the fairing reinforced by Kevlar. Unlike the production versions, the racer had a carbon-fibre airbox, which also increased chassis rigidity. Replacing the analogue instrument panel with a digital type saved a further 3kg.

1994 was the final year that carbon brakes were allowed, and the factory 916 racer had twin Brembo 320mm or 290mm carbon discs on the front, these being shrouded in carbon-fibre covers. At the rear was a 200mm carbon disc. The wheels were three-, or later five-spoke, Marchesini, a 3.50 x 17in on the front with a 6.00 x 17in on the rear. The weight was close to 145kg, and, once the traction problems were solved, the 1994 916 Racing was a formidable machine.

As the racing department was limited in its ability to build many 916 Racing machines during 1994 (14 were constructed), only selected riders received them. The over-the-counter racer for 1994 was still based on the 888 and officially titled the 888 Racing, though it displaced 926cc. On the 916 Racing (actually 955cc), Fabrizio Pirovano rode for Davide Tardozzi, James Whitham for Moto Cinelli, and there were occasional World Superbike

rides for the Australian sensation Troy Corser. Corser had won the 1993 Australian Superbike Championship on an ageing Honda RC30 and earned a ride with Eraldo Ferracci during 1994 in the US AMA Superbike series (on a 955cc engined 1994 888 Racing). Corser proved to be an admirable choice, winning the Championship. He won three races, and team-mate Pascal Picotte, won two.

1995

Ducati was justifiably euphoric after the success of the 916 Racing in its first year of World Superbike competition, and further development of the 955 over the winter saw it even more dominant at the beginning of the 1995 season. Joining Carl Fogarty in the ADVF team run by Virginio Ferrari team was Mauro Lucchiari, but two other teams also received factory support: Alfred Inzinger's Promotor team, managed by Davide Tardozzi, entered Troy Corser and Andreas Meklau, and Fabrizio Pirovano rode a Taurus Ducati entry. Essentially a customer 916 Racing, Pirovano's machine was tuned by Edo Vigna. Whereas the Ferrari team received factory-prepared engines for every race, Vigna

The superb factory 916 of 1995. By the final round of
the World Superbike Championship that year, it featured
Kremlyovskaya vodka sponsorship.

developed his own desmodromic camshafts
and made a number of changes to the engine
specifications. There was still, however, a
considerable difference in power between
the official factory machines and those in
the satellite teams. Only six official factory
916 racers were available, these being the
preserve of Fogarty, Lucchiari, and Corser.
Undoubtedly, Fogarty received the fastest
engines, though Corser seemed to be a
recipient in Austria (home of Promotor), and
Australia. By the final race of the season
in Australia, Virginio Ferrari had signed a
new sponsorship agreement, and the ADVF
sported large Kremlyovskaya Vodka logos.

Engine development concentrated more on
improving reliability rather than outright power.

As crankcase cracking continued to be a
problem, there were stronger crankcases, similar
to before, but without the kickstart boss carried
over from the earlier Pantah design. Menon
provided special nimonic valves (still 37mm and
31mm), and there were revised rockers, special
bronze valve guides and camshafts. Generally,
the 955cc engine (with 11.8:1 96mm Omega
pistons) was employed, but there was also the
occasional use of a larger, 996cc engine with
98mm pistons (in the first and final rounds).
The larger engine didn't produce any more
top-end power, but gave around 12bhp more at
8500rpm. The main reason it wasn't used more
often during the season was that the 955 was
proving more than adequate to win races, and
Fogarty didn't like it. Putting the larger engine

After success in the 1994 AMA Superbike Championship, Troy Corser also made a significant impression during 1995, winning four World Superbike races on the Promotor 916.

in the 955 chassis altered handling, and made it harder to ride. Aiding the rideability of the 955 was a slipper clutch, which also assisted engine braking. As in the previous year, a sensitive KLS electronic shifter was also used. The injection system, with 50mm throttle bodies, was similar to 1994, with a P8 CPU mounted in the fairing in front of the steering head, and separate EPROM mapping for each cylinder. The exhaust headers were 52mm in diameter, and power was 154bhp at 12,000rpm at the crankshaft: this being between 141bhp and 145bhp at the rear wheel. The general improvement of the 1995 955 over that of 1994 was evident in the fact that Fogarty didn't suffer a single mechanical failure all season: his only retirement being due to an electrical fault in Indonesia.

The biggest difference for 1995 was the increase in weight, as required by new regulations, and banning of carbon brakes. Although the initial minimum weight was 147kg (with the 750 fours at 162kg), the success of the Ducati in the first three rounds saw a revision of these weights. Thus, from Monza, the twins were required to weigh in at 155kg, with the 750 fours at 160kg. As the 955 was already at 147kg, a non-functioning starter motor was installed, and lead ballast added under the seat. The brake discs were now steel, with twin 320mm discs on the front, and a 220mm on the rear, along with Brembo P4.32/36 and P2.24 calipers. 46mm Öhlins forks were retained, along with the Öhlins shock absorber. The wheels were five-spoke

Carl Fogarty was totally dominant on the ADVF Ducati 916 during 1995, winning nine races.

Marchesini, a 3.50 x 17in on the front and a 6.25 x 17in on the rear.

For the first time electronic telemetry was run during qualifying, this undoubtedly contributing to the advantage the Ducati exhibited during the season. Another advantage was due to the team employing Anders Andersson as a full-time Öhlins suspension technician. The results were such that, in many ways, the 1995 955 factory racer provided an optimum balance between power, reliability and handling that was difficult to replicate. As the demands of competition required more horsepower, and regulations saw increased weight, future versions of the 916 Racing struggled to match the fine balance of that 1995 model. It wasn't only on the world stage that the 916 dominated that year. In the

UK, Steve Hislop won the British Superbike Championship, and Matt Llewellyn the Shell Advance International Superbike Trophy. In Australia, Shawn Giles won the Australian Shell Masters Series on the Ducati Dealer Team customer 916 Racing. Although former Grand Prix legend Freddie Spencer was recruited to ride the Fast by Ferracci 916 in the AMA Superbike Championship, he couldn't repeat Corser's result of 1994. Spencer won one round, at Monterey, California. This wasn't Spencer's first Ducati experience. Back in 1979 he had performed impressively at Daytona on a Reno Leoni bevel-drive Superbike, almost winning the Superbike race.

During 1995, there was also a modest return to Endurance racing, two special 955 Endurance racers being entered in the Bol

World Superbike Championship victories 1995

World Superbike Champion; Carl Fogarty (Ducati 916)
World Superbike Constructor's Championship; Ducati 916

Date	Circuit	Race	Winner
7 May	Hockenheim, Germany	Race 1 & 2	Carl Fogarty
21 May	Misano, Italy	Race 1 & 2	Mauro Lucchiari
28 May	Donington, GB	Race 1 & 2	Carl Fogarty
18 June	Monza, Rep. San Marino	Race 1	Carl Fogarty
		Race 2	Pierfrancesco Chili
25 June	Albacete, Spain	Race 2	Carl Fogarty
9 July	Salzburgring, Austria	Race 1	Carl Fogarty
		Race 2	Troy Corser
23 July	Laguna Seca, USA	Race 2	Troy Corser
6 August	Brands Hatch, GB	Race 1 & 2	Carl Fogarty
27 August	Sugo, Japan	Race 1	Troy Corser
		Race 2	Carl Fogarty
10 September	Assen, Holland	Race 1 & 2	Carl Fogarty
15 October	Sentul, Indonesia	Race 1	Carl Fogarty
19 October	Phillip Island, Australia	Race 2	Troy Corser

d'Or. Andreas Meklau teamed with Mauro Lucchiari, while Stéphane Chambon put his 955 on pole position. Although the new reinforced crankcases had survived 36 hours on the test bench and promised increased reliability, both the works machines retired.

1996

Although Virginio Ferrari was keen to retain Carl Fogarty as his lead rider, and, right until the final race of 1995, was hopeful, Fogarty departed the Ducati camp to try his luck with the Honda RC45 during 1996. Ferrari then signed the 28-year-old former World 250cc Champion John Kocinski to take his place. Alongside Kocinski was the 22-year-old British rider Neil Hodgson. As Ducati was struggling financially during 1995-96, the ADVF team drew on outside sponsorship, this coming from Kremlyovskaya Vodka. Unfortunately, despite the agreement, the sponsorship money didn't materialise, leaving Ferrari to fund the season by himself with his co-team owner Alfredo Danelli.

Initial testing showed that Kocinski was well suited to the Ducati, further evidenced by his emphatic double victory at the opening World Superbike round at Misano. However, during the season, personality problems surfaced between Kocinski and Ferrari, and, by the end of the season, communication between them was non-existent. This breakdown in their relationship undoubtedly affected the team's performance and morale. Fortunately for Ducati, in addition to the troubled ADVF Virginio Ferrari team, it also supported Troy Corser on the Promotor entry with a full factory machine. Promotor had been the top privateer team in World Superbike during 1995. Six official factory bikes were again constructed, each rider having two at his disposal. Joining Corser in the Promotor team was the

During 1995, Mauro Lucchiari rode the second ADVF 916
and was rewarded with double race wins at Misano.

23-year-old American Mike Hale, although his
equipment wasn't to the same specification
as that of Corser. The Promotor team was still
managed by Davide Tardozzi.

The regulations now required the weight
of the twins to be increased to the same
162kg as the 750cc fours. Thus, the Ducati
engineering team had not only to compensate
for an additional 7kg, but also to match the
improvement of the fours, particularly the
Honda RC45. Developments to the 916 factory
racer for 1996 saw the adoption of a 996cc
engine, though with the 98mm cylinders
only just fitting the crankcases, there were
many more engine failures this year. With the
98mm pistons, the cylinder stud spacing was
limited by the size of the cylinder mouth. Even
reducing the diameter of the cylinder studs
from 8mm to 6mm didn't really provide enough
room for a sufficiently thick cylinder liner. The
liner was only 3mm thick and, as a result, the

normal engine life was only around 1000km.
Corser in particular suffered numerous engine
failures during the season (more than 20).
While the cause of most of these was the
cylinder liner breaking where it entered the
crankcase, many failures were also due to
Corser's penchant for 'wheelies.' This resulted
in reduced oil pressure and subsequent engine
failure and Corser was encouraged to keep his
bravado for the end of the race.

Engine developments saw 54mm throttle
bodies (up from 50mm), these being 48mm
at the butterfly (up from 46mm). The valves
were now a composite design (titanium with
steel at the top of the stem to reduce wear),
but still in the same sizes of 37mm and 31mm.
An important development was the revision of
the previous 31/62 (2:1) primary gears, these
now being 32/59 (1.84:1) to allow for a spread
tooth load. The increase in overall weight also
allowed for thicker crankcase castings, and

John Kocinski replaced Carl Fogarty in the ADVF team for 1996, but the relationship between Kocinski and Virginio Ferrari was troubled.

there was a larger airbox (with larger ducts), the space being created by moving the radiator header tank further forward. The fuel pressure was increased to 5 bar (from 4.5 bar) and with 12:1 three-ring Omega pistons, power was 157bhp at 11,800rpm at the gearbox. Other developments included larger (54mm) diameter exhausts, and a larger water and oil radiator. Because the weight saving was less of a consideration, the engine covers were aluminium rather than magnesium, steel engine bolts employed, and there was even a steel gearbox selector drum.

The power characteristics of the 996 engine for 1996, however, were different to the earlier version, and, despite the increase in capacity, the new engine revved even higher than the earlier 955. Corser admitted to revving to 12,700rpm, and there was no doubting the speed and ability of the 996 that season. Even with the increase in weight, lap times approached that of considerably lighter and

more powerful Grand Prix 500s. At Donington Corser set a new outright lap record of 1 min 33.470 sec (96.281mph; 154.950km/h). To indicate just how good Corser and the 996 were that year, this record stood beyond 2000.

Although there was no longer an extreme emphasis on outright weight minimisation, the most was made of increasing the front weight bias. Thus the triple clamps were now aluminium rather than magnesium, these being adjustable to allow for fork offset between 25mm and 31mm and a choice of trail without changing triple clamps. To keep the rear as light as possible, the same magnesium swingarm as the previous year was used, and carbon-fibre used for everything aft of the centre-line.

A problem caused by the increased power and weight was braking, and for 1996 there were new 46mm Öhlins forks that allowed the brake discs to be spread 28mm further apart for improved cooling. The front Brembo calipers

The 916 (955) Racing 1995-96

For the 1995 model year, the catalogue factory racer was the 916 Racing. As with earlier models, the specification closely followed that of the 1994 official factory bike. Thus the 916 Racing was 955cc, and had identical camshaft timing to the 1994 factory racer, although the inlet camshaft provided more valve lift (12mm). Like the factory bikes, the valve sizes were 37mm and 31mm. As with 1994 888/926 Racing, the IAW injection system featured twin injectors and a 435 (P8) CPU. Also from the 1994 racer came a gearbox with closer ratios. First gear was now 32/16; second 29/18; third 27/20; fourth 25/21; fifth 24/22; sixth; 23/23.The compression ratio was 12:1 and the power 155bhp at 11,500rpm. While this may have seemed optimistic, the 916 Racing proved to be very competitive straight out of the box, Shawn Giles winning at Eastern Creek near Sydney, Australia only days after the 955 was uncrated. In the World Superbike Championship, Pierfrancesco Chili rode a Team Gattolone 916 Racing prepared by Pietro di Gianesin, this being fast enough to win a World Superbike race at Monza.

The chassis specification, too, reflected developments that had proven successful on the track during 1994. Thus the 916 racing had a 10mm longer swingarm than the road bike (giving a wheelbase of 1420mm), and a larger carbon-fibre fuel tank (22 litres). The front suspension was by Öhlins 46mm FG 9650 forks, with an Öhlins DU 5360 rear shock absorber. Braking was full racing specification Brembo, with twin 320mm cast iron discs with P4 32-36mm calipers and a 19mm master cylinder. At the rear was a 200mm disc with a P2 24mm master cylinder and 11mm master cylinder. The wheels were five-spoke Marchesini, a 3.50 x 17in on the front and 6.00 x 17in on the rear. Whereas the street 916 (and 916 SP) now used a frame constructed of ALS 450, the 916 Racing continued with the 25CrMo4 tubing that had featured on the 1994 916 Strada and SP. The weight of the 916 Racing was 154kg and, with production back to normal at Borgo Panigale, 60 955 Racing machines were constructed for 1995.

A further batch of 31 955 Racing machines were constructed for 1996. Although they may have seemed visually identical to the 1995 916 Racing apart from the lack of air vents in the rear tail section, there were a large number of changes. Engine developments saw new crankcases (these not being shared with the 916 SP), aluminium sidecovers, new pistons and conrod bearings. There were also new camshafts, the inlet being patterned on those used on the 1995 factory racers. The exhaust system was enlarged to 52mm, with new mufflers. Other developments included a clutch with a back torque limiter, a steel gearshift selector drum, new timing belts and an oil pump with an enclosed relief valve. With a slightly lower, 11.8:1 compression ratio, power was 153bhp at 11,000rpm.

Chassis developments saw new 46mm Öhlins forks now with a top-out spring, an increase in the thickness of the front brake discs to 6mm, and an aluminium casing and fast preload adjuster for the Öhlins DU 5360 rear shock absorber. The fuel capacity was increased to 23 litres and in line with Superbike regulations, the weight increased to 160kg.

Popular Italian rider, Pierfrancesco Chili, rode the Team Gattolone 916 during 1996, often faster than the works machines.

New weight regulations saw the factory racer for 1996 with aluminium, rather than magnesium, engine covers. Ballast was also used to maintain the weight at 162kg.

were now P4.34/36mm. There was also a new Öhlins rear suspension unit. The wheels were five-spoke magnesium Marchesini: a 3.50 x 17in and 6.00 x 17in. Rather than being employed during qualifying only, a PI System 3 Plus data acquisition system was installed all the time, adding a comfortable 4kg to the overall weight. In addition to the official machines of the Ferrari and Promotor teams, the Gattolone team also received some factory support. However, Pietro di Gianesin did his own engine preparation, unlike the official teams where the engines came fully assembled by the racing department at Borgo Panigale and were returned immediately after the race.

In the World Championship, it was Troy Corser who convincingly gave the Ducati 916 another title with seven emphatic race wins. Kocinski had also performed well on occasion, but was inconsistent. Elsewhere, too, the 916 continued to be victorious. Although the 955cc 916 Racing struggled against the powerful fours in Britain, the US, and Australia, in Europe it was extremely successful. Andreas Meklau won the Austrian Superbike Championship, the Swede Christer Lindholm the German Superbike Championship, and Paolo Casoli the Italian Superbike Championship (on a Gio Ca Moto entry). In the AMA Championship, two young rookies, Larry Pegram and Shawn Higbee, rode for Eraldo Ferracci, but poor results prompted Ducati to enter 1992 125cc World Champion Alessandro Gramigni in four races. Gramigni immediately impressed, winning in the rain at Elkhart Lake, and following this with a victory

World Superbike Championship victories 1996

World Superbike Champion; Troy Corser (Ducati 916)
World Superbike Constructor's Championship; Ducati 916

14 April	Misano, Rep. San Marino	Race 1 & 2	John Kocinski
28 April	Donington, GB	Race 1 & 2	Troy Corser
16 June	Monza, Italy	Race 2	Pierfrancesco Chili
30 June	Brno, Czechoslovakia	Race 1 & 2	Troy Corser
21 July	Laguna Seca, USA	Race 2	John Kocinski
4 August	Brands Hatch, GB	Race 1	Pierfrancesco Chili
		Race 2	Troy Corser
18 August	Sentul, Indonesia	Race 1 & 2	John Kocinski
6 October	Albacete, Spain	Race 1 & 2	Troy Corser

at Brainerd. Gramigni's wins were enough to save face, but not the Championship. Results were also disappointing in the British Superbike Championship. While Terry Rymer on his Old Spice Ducati 955 was the only rider to pose any threat to Yamaha domination, he was called into the Lucky Strike Suzuki Grand Prix team mid-season and missed several rounds. Still, with five victories, he ended third overall in the Championship.

The Australian rider, Troy Corser, gave the Ducati 916 its third successive World Superbike Championship in 1996. Again, Corser rode for the Austrian Promotor team.

1997

With an influx of much needed capital from the TPG buy-in towards the end of 1996, there was an expansion of the World Superbike racing programme for 1997. Not only did the Virginio Ferrari team receive full works support, so, too, did the Andrea Merloni's Gattolone Team, Massimiliano Zani being its chief engineer. Unlike the previous year, Gattolone received engines supplied by the Ducati racing department, these remaining sealed before and after use. Pierfrancesco Chili stayed with the Gattolone Team, but the 1996 champion, Troy Corser, left Superbikes to try his hand (unsuccessfully) in Grand Prix. After a disappointing season on the Honda RC45, Carl Fogarty returned to the Ferrari camp, bringing with him his long-term mechanic, Tony Bass. Neil Hodgson also retained his ride for a second year. Following the failure of the Kremlyovskaya

After deserting the World Superbike Championship in 1997, Corser returned to ride for Ducati in 1998 and 1999.

sponsorship arrangement, there was no outside sponsor for 1997, the factory funding virtually the entire racing budget.

The main development for 1997 was the homologation of new crankcases (via the 916 SPS) with a wider cylinder stud spacing to allow for thicker cylinders with the 98mm pistons of the 996cc engine. As these crankcases were also heavier, there was less need for weight saving and ballast with the 162kg limit. Along with the crankcases were new cylinder heads with larger inlet ports, and a revised combustion chamber. The quest for more horsepower also saw an increase in the throttle body diameter to 60mm, and power up to around 168bhp at 11,300rpm, at the gearbox.

There was also a new gearbox, with a lower first (32/16) and higher second (33/21) gear, a revised exhaust system, and larger capacity oil and water radiators. A slight reshaping of the carbon-fibre and Kevlar fuel tank saw an increase in fuel capacity to 24 litres. There was a new frame, 1.5kg heavier than before, and an even lighter cast magnesium swingarm (2kg) in a further endeavour to get more weight on the front wheel. The 46mm Öhlins forks now had magnesium sliders and a new top out spring, the travel being increased by 5mm to 125mm, and, while the 320mm stainless steel brake discs were still spaced more widely apart for additional cooling, these were 1mm thicker than before. Chili, however, still preferred the earlier, narrower triple clamps. Brembo provided new front brake calipers with larger pistons. The only other change to the chassis specification was a reduction in rear wheel rim width to 5.75 x 17in.

While the engine developments may have aided reliability, 1997 was the first year since 1990 that Ducati failed to win the World Superbike Constructor's Championship. It was also the year that brought a halt to its string of rider's titles since 1994. The reason seemed to be that, finally, Honda had developed its RC45 to a higher level than the 996. The Weber Marelli injection system was still basically the same P8 system that Ducati had been using since 1993. Combined with the new 60mm throttle bodies, and a lighter crankshaft, the increased power and

Fogarty returned to the ADVF team for 1997, but was generally unhappy with the performance of the 996 Ducati. However, he still managed second in the World Superbike Championship.

aggressive response affected handling. There also seemed to be a problem with weight distribution. As ballast was no longer needed, this couldn't be fine-tuned as easily as before, and somehow the balance of the 1996 bike was lost with these developments. What had started life as a 146kg 916 with about 140 rear wheel bhp, had evolved into a 162kg 996 with 154 rear wheel bhp. With this evolution came a change in the character of the machine, and it was much more difficult to ride. During the season, a number of new features were tried, including even longer swingarms, smaller (290mm) front brake discs to quicken steering response, and a higher profile Michelin rear tyre.

Even after consistent development, Carl Fogarty was generally unhappy with the

996, openly stating that he preferred his 1995 955. Often his race and lap times were slower than they had been in 1995, but he still managed second place in the World Superbike Championship. When Fogarty crashed at Albacete, he lost the Championship to John Kocinski. Chili, too, complained about the power delivery and, for Brands Hatch, was provided with a new EPROM that gave less aggressive power delivery. This improved handling so much that he won the first race, and might have even won the second if Fogarty hadn't taken him down during the race.

In the British Superbike Championship, two teams fronted with braces of customer 996 Racing machines. In the Reve Red Bull team, managed by Roger Marshall, John Reynolds teamed with Steve Hislop, while

Returning for a second season with the ADVF team was the young British rider Neil Hodgson. His results were disappointing during 1997, and he would have to wait until 2000 before his talent could be realised.

There were new crankcases for the 996 for 1997, and 60mm throttles, but the aggressive power delivery affected handling.

Although the style of the factory racer was similar, the 1997 version featured a re-shaped fuel tank.

Colin Seeley managed the GSE (Groundwork South East) Ducati team, with Sean Emmett as rider. Reynolds won two races, Emmett one, and Ian Simpson (replacing a sacked Hislop) another. However, the Ducatis were completely overwhelmed by the Yamaha of Niall McKenzie in this Championship.

Things weren't much better in the US, though it looked very promising initially. Eraldo Ferracci signed Australian Matthew Mladin after an impressive AMA debut year in 1996 on the Suzuki. Joining Mladin was Gerald Rothman Jnr. This year also saw the formation of the Vance & Hines Ducati team after it lost its Yamaha contract. Vance & Hines hired Thomas Stevens, also recruiting Christer

Lindholm for the final race. After a promising start to the season, a DNF at Daytona effectively ruined his Championship. Mladin won four races, but could still only manage third in the Championship. Fortunately for Ducati, Andreas Meklau continued his winning ways in the Austrian Superbike Championship and, as usual, Ducati dominated in Italy. Here Serafino Foti won the Italian Superbike Championship with two race wins. However, despite the new 996, 1997 was the least successful year for Ducatis in national and international Superbike racing since 1990. Fortunately, the technicians worked hard over the winter and for 1998 produced an improved machine.

World Superbike Championship victories 1997

20 April	Misano, Rep. San Marino	Race 1	Pierfrancesco Chili
4 May	Donington, GB	Race 2	Carl Fogarty
8 June	Hockenheim, Germany	Race 2	Carl Fogarty
22 June	Monza, Italy	Race 2	Pierfrancesco Chili
3 August	Brands Hatch, GB	Race 1	Pierfrancesco Chili
		Race 2	Carl Fogarty
17 August	Zeltweg, Austria	Race 1	Carl Fogarty
31 August	Assen, Holland	Race 2	Carl Fogarty
12 October	Sentul, Indonesia	Race 2	Carl Fogarty

1998

The loss of both the riders' and constructors' titles in the 1997 World Superbike Championship prompted Ducati to expand its official programme for 1998 and develop the 996 racer to a new level. Its stated aim for 1998 was to win three Championships, the World Superbike, World Supersport, and AMA Superbike. A total of 18 factory 996 racers were built, and, for the World Superbike Championship, three riders were supported in two official teams. After a disappointing year in 500cc Grand Prix, Troy Corser was again signed to ride a factory machine, with Fogarty initially linked to a number of potential sponsors. After a deal with the Belgian Alstare Corona team fell through, it looked like Fogarty would either join Corser in the ADVF Virginio Ferrari team, or Chili in the Gattolone team. Then, in early January 1998, it was announced that Ducati Motor would fully support a new team, Team Ducati Performance, as part of its promotion of the Gio Ca Moto range of performance accessories for the series production Ducati motorcycles.

Team Ducati Performance consisted of two riders; Carl Fogarty contesting the World Superbike Championship, with Paolo Casoli attempting to regain the Supersport World Cup

he won in 1997 on the Gio Ca Moto 748 SP. Managing the team was Davide Tardozzi, who had been with Troy Corser at Promotor in 1996. There were also new mechanics for Fogarty, although he came with his own personal mechanic, Tony Bass. Alongside Team Ducati Performance was Virginio Ferrari's ADVF team of two riders as before, these now being Troy Corser and Pierfrancesco Chili. As usual, long time Ducati racer and technician Franco Farnè was the team's technical director. Both the Ducati Performance and ADVF teams were on an equal footing, receiving full factory machines, and there were no official orders as to which rider should win a race.

Realising the importance of World Superbike racing, Ducati reorganised the racing department at Bologna, and doubled its investment in the programme. With more resources at its disposal, Claudio Domenicali's racing department worked hard over the winter to improve the 996 racer. Developments were aimed at altering the weight distribution and power delivery so that handling replicated the all-conquering 155kg 955cc machine of 1995. Thus, in off-season testing, smaller inlet valves and a remapped ignition system were trialled. Chassis experimentation included various swingarms and revised fork triple clamp and chassis settings. By the time the specification of the 1998 racer was finalised, it was a

The 996 Racing 1997-98

An even smaller number of 996 Racing machines (20) were produced for 1997, these reflecting the developments on the factory machines during 1996. The crankcases were the newly homologated 916 SPS type and the engine displaced 996cc. With 98mm 12:1 pistons, power was 155bhp at 11,000rpm. There was a new exhaust camshaft, new valve rocker arms, and, in line with the 1996 factory bikes, a 32/59 tooth primary drive instead of the suspect 31/62. Also from the 1996 factory bikes came an increase in the fuel pressure to 5 bar. There was a larger capacity airbox, a larger oil radiator, and 54mm exhaust headers. The injection system was the same P8 system as on the earlier 916 Racing. Chassis developments saw the adjustable offset triple clamps that had been successfully used during 1996, thicker (6mm) front brake discs, a larger air intake in the front fairing, and altered handlebar and rear wheel hub assembly. Again these over-the-counter racers were entered in the major national Superbike Championships around the world, but were not as successful as in past years.

For 1998, the 916 Racing was again produced in small numbers (24), with several important developments to keep it competitive. As usual, the general specification was that of the factory machines in the previous year, and there were a number of engine modifications and frame modifications. Although most of the 1997 engine specification was retained, there was a new crankshaft and conrod assembly, along with an improved primary drive and spline coupling. Small developments to aid reliability saw different crankshaft shimming, a new crankshaft inlet oil seal, bigger rimmed timing belt rollers, and a larger capacity water radiator. The radiator had three extra rows as well as being thicker. There was a new gearshift drum to help smooth out the gearshift, and, as with the 1997 factory machine, a 60mm throttle body with new inlet manifolds. Although the works machines had experienced difficulties during 1997, running the large 60mm throttles with the twin injector P8 injection system, the 1998 916 Racing persevered with this system. To improve reliability in wet races, the control unit in the front fairing featured better water-proofing. Valve sizes remained at 37mm and 31mm, and the claimed power was less than for 1997, at 151bhp at 11,000rpm.

The chassis came in for even more development for 1998, with a TIG-welded frame in 25CrMo4, using 1.5mm tubing, along with a lighter rear subframe. The 46mm Öhlins fork, too, was similar to that of the 1997 factory bike, with the same axle lugs. In addition to the standard 320mm front discs came optional 290mm discs. The rear Öhlins shock absorber also featured hydraulic adjustment for the spring preload. Also in line with the factory bikes was a larger, and reshaped, 24-litre fuel tank. A longer magnesium swingarm increased the wheelbase to 1430mm, also having the effect of improving the weight distribution. The weight, too, was lower, at 154kg, so further fine tuning of the weight distribution could be accomplished through ballast.

However, the performance of these 1998 916 Racing machines remained disappointing. There was still an enormous gap between them and the official machines, which became even more marked after the homologation of a new frame mid-season. What was really needed for the various national Championships was a machine closer in specification to that of the official factory racers. This happened in 1999 with the 996 RS, and results immediately improved.

A line-up of 1998 916 Racing machines awaiting dispatch at the factory in January 1998.

significantly changed, and improved, machine over the 1997 version.

Engine development saw a new electronic injection system, the long-serving P8 being replaced by a new Magnetti Marelli MF3-S system derived from Ferrari Formula One practice. A major advantage of the new system was the ability of mechanics to download data through a laptop connected to the onboard computer, via a Marelli DAS3 data acquisition system. It was now also possible to modify EFI settings through the external laptop, rather than by substituting a pre-mapped EPROM as before. Retaining the 60mm throttle bodies, the MF3-S system also incorporated a third injector. Along with two Marelli IW724 injectors was a third competition-type Marelli IWF1. These additional injectors were located outboard from each velocity-stack opening and closer to the airbox. Only operating at 70% to full throttle when the primary injectors were shut off, because they were positioned further from the inlet valve they made for cooler, and denser, air entering the combustion chamber. Along with the new injection system, there were redesigned air intakes and airbox, the aim being to further improve cylinder filling with colder air. There was also a redesigned Termignoni exhaust system, with reverse cones incorporated in the mufflers. The result was an increase in power to between 163bhp and 165bhp at 12,000rpm, but reliability still left room for improvement and there were a few engine problems throughout the season.

It wasn't only the engine that came in for serious development. In an endeavour to solve the problems of the front end pushing that had plagued all the riders during 1997, the engine was located slightly more forward in the chrome-molybdenum 25CrMo4 frame. This was also claimed to be slightly less stiff than previously, so as not to exaggerate suspension flaws. There was increased sophistication in

Former racer Davide Tardozzi managed the new Ducati Performance team for 1998. Tardozzi came with impressive credentials, having been behind Corser's 1996 World Superbike Championship.

the development of the suspension for 1998. For the first time, Grand Prix-quality equipment was available from Öhlins, the 46mm forks now having magnesium sliders (as on the Yamaha 500cc Grand Prix machines) and totally different internals. The triple clamps provided offset between 25mm and 30mm. At the rear, a new Öhlins TT44 rear suspension unit was tried, and used at some rounds, although Fogarty generally favoured the 1997 shock absorber. The TT44 featured 'double tube' technology from Formula One and Indy car racing, and used separate twin internal oil tubes for compression and rebound damping. These also offered a wider range of settings. The Brembo brakes were a development of those in 1997, with a choice of two- or four-pad front brake calipers, and either 320mm or

In addition to the Ducati Performance team, there was also Virginio Ferrari's ADVF team, with riders Chili and Corser.

290mm steel discs. The quest for improved steering and traction also saw experimentation with different wheel sizes, including a 16in front Marchesini, and 17in, in rim widths of 3.25in, 3.50in, and 3.75in. At the rear was either a 6.00 x 16.5in or 5.75 x 17in wheel, although Fogarty experimented with a one-off 6.25 x 16.5in Marchesini after tyre problems at Phillip Island. The wheelbase of the 1998 996 was 1430mm, and the improvement in weight distribution saw 53-54% on the front wheel, and 46-47% on the rear wheel.

Although the 1998 996 was immediately an improvement over the 1997 bike, it still lacked power compared to the opposition. Early season results, though, were encouraging, especially after Fogarty won the first race of the year, but the dominance that Ducati was looking for eluded it. However, a significant development occurred for the South African round at Kyalami in early July. A newly homologated frame (through the 916 SPS

Fogarty Replica) allowed the rear bracing tube to be moved back and downwards. This also located the engine slightly lower than before. Even more important, though, was the alteration of one of the top transverse frame tubes under the fuel tank to create a larger capacity airbox and revised air intake with shorter intakes. These were now completely inside the airbox. Combined with new camshafts and a different valve angle to improve fuel delivery, these developments improved the 996 racer dramatically. The torque curve became flatter, there was even more top-end power (reputedly 7-8bhp), and this had a beneficial influence on handling. Although it seemed a simple modification, this new frame provided the single most effective development of the 996 in recent years, and, at the first Kyalami race, Ducatis filled the first three places.

Despite these developments, it was still a tough year for both Fogarty and Ducati, and,

Engine developments on the factory 996 for 1998 saw a new Weber MF3-S triple injector EFI. Later in the season, there was a new frame and airbox.

by mid-season, Fogarty's hopes of winning the title looked bleak. Following this mid-year crisis, a victory at Assen, and then Corser's crash in the warm-up at the final event at Sugo, allowed Fogarty to take his third world title for Ducati by only 4.5 points. The only sourness of the season was after the second race at Assen, when there was a confrontation between Fogarty and Chili. The involvement of Virginio Ferrari in this fracas also seemed to cause some bitterness, and possibly influenced future team developments.

Filling out the World Superbike grid was, again, the Andrea Merloni-owned Gattolone Team, this now being a privateer outfit and a shadow of its former self. With 29-year-old Alessandro Gramigni riding, it struggled even to finish in the points. More successful was the De Cecco Ducati of Spanish rider Gregorio Lavilla. With a customer 916 Racing and engines built

by noted engine builder Nando De Cecco, Lavilla impressed with two podium finishes during the season.

It wasn't only in the World Superbike Championship that activities were expanded. After a fairly horrific year in all the premier national Superbike series, a more concerted attempt was made, particularly in the US. With TPG being a US company and Ducati now seeing its future sales growth being led by the previously slow US market, there were now two officially supported Superbike teams for the AMA Superbike Championship. Riding for Eraldo Ferracci was previous Ducati World Superbike rider (Promotor in 1996) Mike Hale, with Tom Kipp on a second machine. Vance & Hines again received factory support and former Kawasaki World Superbike rider Anthony Gobert joined Thomas Stevens. Gobert came with a reputation as an extremely

Troy Corser's 1998 factory 996 looked very similar to the
1997 version, but provided improved performance.

talented, but wild and undisciplined, rider and
it was hoped he could give Ducati the AMA
Superbike title that had proved so elusive
since 1994. Thus, Gobert received a factory
machine, although AMA regulations required
54mm throttle bodies (rather than 60mm). Initial
testing at Daytona looked promising: Gobert
set the fastest preliminary times, and then had
a win in the opening round at Phoenix. He
followed this with victories at Road Atlanta and
Road America. However, while Gobert could
undoubtedly win races, his erratic behaviour
and his failure of two drug tests during the
season saw him finish a lowly ninth in the
Championship. Yet, while Gobert, and stand-in
Vance & Hines rider Jason Pridmore, achieved
some good results, it was a particularly lean
year for the Ferracci team; Kipp managing only
one podium finish.

In England the Red Bull Ducati squad was
expanded, Sean Emmett leaving the GSE
team to ride alongside John Reynolds. On the
strength of impressive rides in World Superbike
races at Phillip Island, former Australian Suzuki
Superbike rider Troy Bayliss was drafted into
Team GSE, partnering Jamie Robinson. Due to
injury, though, there were a number of changes
in the riders' line-up of these teams during the
season. Matt Llewellyn rode first for the Red
Bull team, before replacing Robinson in the
GSE line-up. While the British Championship
machines were ostensibly customer 916
Racing, the two teams did receive some factory
support. By mid-season, both teams had
the Weber MF3-S triple injector system. Yet,
despite having four riders competing in the
British Superbike Championship, this remained
a series that eluded Ducati.

World Superbike Championship victories 1998

World Superbike Champion; Carl Fogarty (Ducati 996)
World Superbike Constructor's Championship; Ducati 996

22 March	Phillip Island, Australia	Race 1	Carl Fogarty
24 May	Albacete, Spain	Race 1	Pierfrancesco Chili
		Race 2	Carl Fogarty
7 June	Nürburgring, Germany	Race 2	Pierfrancesco Chili
5 July	Kyalami, South Africa	Race 1 & 2	Pierfrancesco Chili
12 July	Laguna Seca, USA	Race 1	Troy Corser
2 August	Brands Hatch, GB	Race 2	Troy Corser
6 September	Assen, Holland	Race 1	Pierfrancesco Chili
		Race 2	Carl Fogarty

Although mid-way through the season Fogarty had almost conceded the Championship, he eventually won by the barest of margins.

For the 1998 British Superbike Championship,
Troy Bayliss was drafted into the GSE Racing team.

There were some good individual results, Bayliss, Emmett, Llewellyn and Reynolds each winning races, but the best overall result was Reynolds' fourth in the Championship. However, Ducati still performed well in the Italian and German Superbike Championships: Paolo Blora won in Italy, and Andreas Meklau in Germany.

1999

After Carl Fogarty's astounding victory in the 1998 World Superbike Championship, the entire Ducati racing programme was revamped for 1999. Central to this was the establishment of a new company, Ducati Corse, entirely owned by Ducati Motor, but controlling all the official racing operations in four different Championships. In addition to World Superbike, these were the AMA Superbike

Championship, World Supersport, and the Italian Superbike Championship. There was also more serious factory involvement in other Championships, with a higher specification 996 Racing Special replacing the previous 996 Racing. Directing Ducati Corse was Claudio Domenicali, an engineer often considered the heir apparent to Massimo Bordi, overseeing an operating budget of US$11 million.

There was now only one official team in World Superbike, Team Ducati Performance, and this saw the departure of several Ducati icons of the past, notably Franco Farnè, Virginio Ferrari and Pierfrancesco Chili. After an association with Ducati since 1954, and involvement with every racing Ducati since that date, Farnè left to be a mechanic with Marco Lucchinelli's R&D Team, although he remained a development consultant for Ducati Corse. The sacking of Virginio Ferrari was particularly acrimonious, and, although Ducati chief

Federico Minoli was personally in favour of retaining Chili as a supporting rider to Fogarty, he went in favour of Troy Corser. Maintaining his position, though, was team manager Davide Tardozzi, and much of the success of the team during 1999 was undoubtedly attributable to Tardozzi's abilities.

For its retention of the World Superbike title, Ducati made use of the pre-season homologation rules to cast new cylinder heads for the 996. The increased thickness allowed for improved engine rigidity and enhanced porting, and there were slightly re-angled valves. Also homologated for 1999 were a new airbox and intake tracts. Engine development saw new camshafts, but the same triple injector MF3-S system with differential mapping between the cylinders. The rider could also select two different programs, if required. There was a choice of two different gearboxes, the Evolution gearbox having taller first and second gears. However, without a cassette-style gearbox, experimentation with different internal ratios required complete engine substitution. During the season, the stainless steel exhaust system diameter was increased to 57mm (from 54mm) and the claimed power was 168bhp at 11,500rpm. Although power was also said to be 7bhp more than in 1998, this figure was undoubtedly a conservative one. As always there was considerable inconsistency in the quoted power outputs given by the racing department, but, given the results during the season, the factory machine certainly wasn't lacking in horsepower during 1999. The biggest advance from 1998 wasn't so much the increase in peak power, but the improvement throughout the range, with less power drop off. There was also a noticeable increase in engine reliability this year, with no DNFs from engine failure.

After the breakthrough of 1998 with the new frame and airbox, most development was centred on improving the chassis. In an effort to replicate the rider-friendly 1995 955, Fogarty went to smaller diameter (42mm) Öhlins front forks. While reducing the front end stiffness, they improved the feel from the front tyre, as well as reducing unsprung weight. Along with the narrower forks came a new Öhlins TT44 shock absorber (with all new hydraulics) and a revision of the rear suspension linkage. In an endeavour to reduce the rear wheel chatter that had been a problem during 1998, the rear suspension linkage now featured a constant-rate 2:1 rather than a rising-rate. With the new forks came Brembo radial four-piston brake calipers, similar to those that had featured on a number of Grand Prix machines during 1998. These were more rigidly located on the fork slider, improving braking action. With 290mm discs, there was also reduced front rotating mass and steering response improved, although, on occasion, 320mm discs were still used. As part of the continuous evolution of this great design, a smaller fuel tank was homologated, this extending more into the airbox, as well as being slimmer and 20mm lower to improve aerodynamics. The wheelbase, too, was slightly shorter at 1425mm.

From the first race of the season, it became evident that the development work over the off-season had been successful. This, combined with Fogarty's undoubted psychological advantage, saw him comfortably win both races at Kyalami. From this point on, the opposition never recovered, and Fogarty had wrapped up his fourth title by the penultimate round in Hockenheim. With eleven race wins, Fogarty was almost as dominant as he had been during that most memorable of years, 1995. On top of this, Corser took three victories, and the Vance & Hines duo of Anthony Gobert and Ben Bostrom a win apiece at Laguna Seca. Ducati ended up winning more races than all the other teams combined. Its policy of focused evolution was paying off handsomely.

There was only one official factory team for 1999, Team
Ducati Performance. Developments saw thinner front
forks and radial Brembo brake calipers. In the hands
of Fogarty, this machine was almost as dominant as in
1995.

In addition to the World Superbike
Championship, there was another concerted
effort mounted in the US during 1999.
Receiving full factory support were the two
AMA Superbike teams of Vance & Hines
and Eraldo Ferracci. The machines were
1999 specification 996 Factory, although
with 54mm throttle bodies, as required by the
AMA regulations. However, the set-ups of the
machines differed, with Dunlop tyres being
used rather than Michelin, and 46mm Öhlins
forks with normal racing Brembo calipers.
Anthony Gobert was given another chance
on the Vance & Hines bike, his team-mate for
1999 being number one AMA plate holder, Ben
Bostrom. Matt Wait joined Larry Pegram on
the Ferracci machines. On paper, the Vance &
Hines team looked the strongest, and Bostrom
looked as though he might take his second
AMA Championships title. However, it was only
after his uplifting performance at the World
Superbike race at Laguna Seca, that Bostrom
went on to win an AMA race, at Brainerd.

Gobert, for all his brilliance, was erratic again.
He won five races (more than any other rider),
but failed to show up for the final event of the
season, and ended fourth in the Championship.
This lack of support for team-mate Bostrom
effectively ended Gobert's career with Ducati.
For a rider who could have been groomed to
replace Fogarty, it was an ignominious end.
As a consolation, though, Ducati did win the
manufacturer's title.

Although, again, Ducati failed in its quest
for the AMA title, there was success in the
British, Australian, and Italian Superbike
Championships. Ducati Corse now provided
more direct support for the British and
Australian Championships and, with higher
specification 996 Racing Specials, the results
were immediately improved. In the British
series, two teams were supported, these still
being the Reve Red Bull and Colin Wright's
INS/GSE Racing team. The riders were largely
unchanged, Emmett and Reynolds staying
with the Red Bull team, though former ADVF

World Superbike Championship victories 1999

World Superbike Champion; Carl Fogarty (Ducati 996)
World Superbike Constructor's Championship; Ducati 996

28 March	Kyalami, South Africa	Race 1 & 2	Carl Fogarty
18 April	Phillip Island, Australia	Race 1 & 2	Troy Corser
2 May	Donington Park, GB	Race 1	Carl Fogarty
30 May	Monza, Italy	Race 1 & 2	Carl Fogarty
13 June	Nürburgring, Germany	Race 1	Carl Fogarty
		Race 2	Troy Corser
27 June	Misano, Rep. San Marino	Race 1 & 2	Carl Fogarty
11 July	Laguna Seca, USA	Race 1	Anthony Gobert
		Race 2	Ben Bostrom
5 September	Assen, Holland	Race 1 & 2	Carl Fogarty
12 September	Hockenheim, Germany	Race 1	Carl Fogarty

rider Neil Hodgson joined Bayliss in the INS/GSE team. These two teams were also contracted to ride in four World Superbike races. The improvement of the 996 RS became evident right from the first round of the British Superbike Championship, when Hodgson won. Bayliss then went on to take the Championship, with seven victories, although all the Ducati riders shared in the spoils, and Ducati won 17 of the 24 races. The Ducati Dealer Team in Australia also received two 996 Racing Specials, the riders being Steve Martin and Craig Connell. After many attempts, Steve Martin finally gave Ducati the Australian Superbike Championship. Other 996 RSs were supplied to the Remus Racing Team for Andreas Meklau in the German Pro Superbike Championship, and two supporting teams in the World Superbike Championship. These were for Lucio Pedercini and Lucchinelli's R&D Team of Doriano Romboni, but their performances were disappointing.

With Paolo Casoli as the official Ducati Corse testing and development rider, the 996 Factory evolution machine completely dominated the Italian Superbike Championship, Casoli winning all four rounds. Casoli's

996 was a test bed machine for the World Superbike racers and featured a number of developments. Central to this was a single injector fuel-injection system, with the throttle butterfly still closer to the valves and allowing for an even shorter intake. However, as the factory racer of Fogarty was proving so dominant, these modifications were kept for the 2000 season.

2000

After the complete dominance of Carl Fogarty during 1999, the 2000 season initially looked promising. However, events showed that not only was Carl Fogarty crucial to Ducati's success, he was also a difficult rider to replace if injured. While the 1999 racing season had exceeded any of Ducati's expectations, the 2000 competition year was one of early disappointment. Despite the appearance of the new Honda RC51, the 996 Factory racer was still competitive, but Ducati Corse made some errors of judgement in the team personnel. The result was that the year 2000 saw fewer victories in a season for Ducati than ever

Despite taking three race victories and finishing third
in the 1999 World Superbike Championship, Troy
Corser was unceremoniously dumped from the Ducati
Performance team for the 2000 season.

before in the World Superbike Championship.
However, as Ducati Corse Chief Engineer
Corrado Cecchinelli said to the author, "It is not
good to always win, and increased competition
makes for a better Championship."

Renewing its collaboration with the Italian
telecommunications company Infostrada,
the official team was now called Team
Ducati Infostrada. Still managed by Davide
Tardozzi, a surprise to many observers was
the controversial sacking of Troy Corser at
the end of the 1999 season. This saw former
AMA Superbike champion 25-year-old Ben
Bostrom joining Carl Fogarty in the 2000
line-up. Fogarty retained the No 1 plate, while
Bostrom used 155, the Infostrada customer
care number. Alongside the two Superbikes
were two official factory 748 RS Supersport
machines, ridden by Paolo Casoli (Number

15) and Ruben Xaus (Number 5). This number
combination also gave the 155 Infostrada
number. Other personnel changes saw the
departure of Fogarty's long-term mechanic,
Anthony Bass. As during 1999, factory support
was also supplied to teams using the 996 RS.
These included the Ducati NCR team of Juan
Borja and Lance Isaacs, the R&D Bieffe Team
with Haruchika Aoki, and the Gerin Red Bull
Team of Andreas Meklau and Robert Ulm.

Ducati Corse produced an improved
machine for the 2000 season, the biggest
changes being to the injection system. Still
retaining the Marelli MF3-S CPU and 60mm
throttle bodies, the triple injector system was
discarded. Paolo Casoli tested a single injector
during 1999 on the 996 Factory evolution,
but as the 1999 996 Factory was proving
so dominant, this was not raced in World

The 996 Racing Special

Reflecting the increased emphasis Ducati was placing on other Championships besides World Superbike, was production of a higher specification racer in addition to the 996 Racing. This 996 Racing Special incorporated many features of the highly successful 1998 factory bike, and was immediately a more competitive machine than its predecessor. The most important developments centred around the use of a similar MF3-S electronic injection system (with 60mm throttle bodies and three injectors) and the revised frame with the larger airbox. This also allowed the throttle bodies to be totally inside the airbox rather than just the bellmouths. The 996 RS had larger titanium valves (39mm inlet and 32mm exhaust), factory ported cylinder heads, shorter inlet tracts and a higher lift inlet camshaft (13mm instead of 12mm). In other respects, the engine was similar to before, including the same racing crankshaft with splined rather than tapered press-fit primary drive. Also from the previous model came the Pankl titanium conrods, and Omega pistons, although the slipper clutch had an aluminium centre rather than steel. The exhaust system was the same, although the Termignoni mufflers were shorter. As with all the racing versions, there was a magnesium sump extension with the oil pick up at the bottom, the lubrication system upgraded to pump 3.3 litres of oil per minute (rather than the 2.6 litres for the street bike). Although no power was claimed, the 996 RS produced around 7-8 more peak horsepower, but with more noticeable gains in the mid-range. Along with the higher specification engine came the newly homologated frame and upgraded specification Brembo brakes and Öhlins suspension. The front Brembo brake calipers were the four-pad type, and the forks 46mm FG 8750S, with a DV 7290 rear shock absorber. With only 11 996 RSs produced they were however in short supply. Unlike the official Ducati Performance factory machines that were supplied with Ducati Corse-assembled engines for each meeting, most of the preparation of the 996 RS was left to the individual teams. Thus, as raced, the specification of the various 996 RSs differed slightly. Additionally for 1999, a slightly lower specification 996 Racing was also available, although only six were produced. The main difference between the 996 Racing Special and 996 Racing was in the injection system. The 996 Racing retained the twin injector IAW P8 CPU, this however being a revised 442 (instead of 435) unit. The

442 CPU was then offered as replacement for all 435 units, as fitted to the 916 SP and 996 SPS.

There was a further batch of ten 996 Racing Special produced for 2000 for selected teams in the World Superbike and various national Championships. The specification of these included many of the developments that had appeared on the 996 Factory during 1999, including the revised single injector MF3-S Marelli injection system and larger diameter (57mm) stainless steel exhaust system. These 996 RS 2000 were surprisingly close in performance to the official Team Ducati Infostrada machines, evidenced by Bostrom's performances on the NCR entry in the 2000 World Superbike Championship. They also featured similar Öhlins 42mm forks and radial caliper Brembo front brakes. The 996 RS as raced by Hodgson used 46mm Öhlins forks, with slightly longer tubes than in 1999, and AP six-piston front brake calipers with 320mm discs.

Neil Hodgson not only performed brilliantly in the British Superbike Championship on the 2000 model 996 RS, he also won two World Superbike races.

Fogarty raced in only two rounds during 2000 before crashing out in Australia. Without him, Ducati had difficulty emulating the excellent results of previous years.

Superbike. According to Corrado Cecchinelli, "The single injector was a simpler solution and allowed more freedom with the shape of the intake manifold. Also, with the three injectors, it was difficult to correctly map the lower part of the power delivery. It was always the intention to go for a single injector, but in 1998 the power delivery wasn't as good and we were more comfortable with three injectors. The move to a single injector was relatively easy, because the three injectors never worked simultaneously, only either the bottom two or the top injector that worked at low or high settings." A bonus with the single injector positioned above the throttle valve was the ability to alter the distance between the injector and the valve. Shorter or longer bellmouths could also be used, depending on the power requirements for individual tracks, but, at this stage, there were no variable length intakes.

Homologated for 2000 through the 996 Factory Replica 2 were new cylinder heads with more material around the studs, to cure head gasket sealing problems and improve stiffness. These new heads also provided more material around the ports, allowing for easier modification of the ports and also leaving room for future development. The valve sizes remained at 39mm inlet and 32mm exhaust and there were new desmodromic camshafts. One of the reasons that the twin cylinder Ducati had remained competitive for so long was undoubtedly the continued development of the desmodromic system. Ducati was still the only company committed to such a valve operating system, and was reaping the benefits of many years of development. The advantages of fully controlled opening and closing valve cycles, especially when combined with advanced computer design programs, undeniably contributed to the excellent power characteristics of the 996cc engine.

The compression ratio with the 98mm

pistons was higher, "very high" according to Cecchinelli, and this was combined with even shorter intakes than in 1999. With special fuel developed by Shell, these developments saw a modest power increase of around 5bhp to 168bhp at 12,000rpm, the rev limiter being set at 12,500rpm. Considering that the claimed power in 1999 was also 168bhp, there was definitely some inconsistency in the power claims. However, Cecchinelli said "We have managed to increase the power of the engine about five horsepower per year over the past three years, a 15 horsepower increase purely through evolution." A noticeable change for 2000 was the use of titanium (rather than carbon-fibre) Termignoni mufflers, these being the same weight, but offering improved durability. Although the new 998cc engine was waiting in the wings, the new castings allowed for the continuous evolution of the 996 throughout the season.

Chassis evolution saw revisions to the internal cartridge of the 42mm Öhlins forks, and different internal bleeding for the Öhlins shock absorber. The Marchesini wheels were still 17in front, and either 17in or 16.5in on the rear. The overall weight of the machine was reduced, so lead needed to be added to the swingarm pivot to maintain the 162kg minimum. Early testing saw experimentation with a double-sided swingarm, with high-exiting exhausts similar to an 888, but these experiments proved inconclusive, and the single-sided swingarm was retained. This was 15mm longer than that of the road bike, giving a wheelbase of 1425mm. There was also an updated Magneti Marelli data acquisition system, with more channels and memory increased to 24MB (up from 2MB).

On paper, the Team Ducati Infostrada combination of riders looked extremely strong, but the reality was that the team was very dependent on Fogarty. By the beginning of the 2000 season, Fogarty had 59 victories to his

Developments to the 996 racer for 2000 included a
single fuel injector per cylinder and titanium mufflers.

name (55 on a Ducati) and was by far the most
successful rider ever in this Championship. So
when Fogarty crashed out in Australia, badly
breaking his left arm, Bostrom wasn't ready to
assume the role of lead rider. In early testing,
Bostrom experienced some difficulty adjusting
to the Michelin tyres (from Dunlop) and wasn't
happy with the Brembo radial front brake set-
up. He reverted to the older style brake calipers
and mounting system, but still struggled. In the
first five rounds, his best result was a seventh
place and, after the fifth round at Monza,
he was demoted to the satellite Ducati NCR
team on a 996 RS. Borja took his place with
Team Infostrada Ducati. Strangely, Bostrom's
performances immediately improved following
this demotion, with several podium finishes
ahead of the Team Infostrada machines. It
seemed that Bostrom's demotion coincided
with his adjustment to both the Michelin tyres
and radial front brake set-up.

Fogarty's replacement in the Team Ducati

Infostrada for the Japanese round at Sugo
was the 31-year-old Australian Troy Bayliss.
Drafted in from the AMA Championship,
Bayliss crashed out, leading to Luca Cadalora,
engaged in testing the 998 replacement for the
2001 season, riding at Donington. Cadalora's
failure then led to Bayliss again joining the
team for Monza. Excellent performances in
Monza and Hockenheim, saw him signed
for the rest of the season, despite being
contracted to Vance & Hines in the US. Borja,
too, retained his ride for the rest of the 2000
season. The surprise performances, though,
were from former works rider Neil Hodgson on
the GSE racing 996 RS. Hodgson seemed to
come of age in 2000, winning two races and
gaining two podium finishes in his six starts.

However, the 2000 season remained one
of the most disappointing for Ducati since the
inception of the series in 1988. The 996 only
mounted the top of the podium four times,
but despite a dearth of victories, the sheer

World Superbike Championship victories 2000

14 May	Donington Park, GB	Race 2	Neil Hodgson
4 June	Hockenheim, Germany	Race 1	Troy Bayliss
6 August	Brands Hatch, GB	Race 1	Troy Bayliss
		Race 2	Neil Hodgson
15 October	Brands Hatch	Race 1	John Reynolds

number of Ducatis on the grid ensured that, again, Ducati won the constructor's title. This rather unpublicised and overshadowed title still showed that the 996 racer was far from dead, despite the advent of the new Honda RC 51.

In other Championships, Ducati Corse continued to provide equipment and support. Fresh from his success in Britain, Troy Bayliss was signed, along with Steve Rapp, to ride for the Vance & Hines team in the AMA Superbike Championship. There was no longer a Fast by Ferracci Ducati Team, Larry Pegram now riding for Tim Pritchard's Ohio-based Competition Accessories on a leased 996 RS. However, Ferracci still had some involvement in the bike's preparation. Bayliss immediately impressed by setting pole position at Daytona, although he crashed during the race while dicing for the lead. When Bayliss was called to the World Superbike Team Ducati Infostrada, former Ducati Superbike rider John Kocinski took his place in the Vance & Hines team for the AMA Championship. The US 996 racing machines also used a single injector system, but different rules required 54mm throttle bodies. The engines were otherwise the same, but for standard cylinder head castings. However, results were poor, and the Kocinski relationship unsuccessful, and during July 2000 Ducati Corse announced it would be discontinuing its relationship with Vance & Hines for 2001.

Following its success in the 1999 British Superbike Championship, Ducati again mounted a concerted effort to win in 2000, and 996 RSs were supplied to two teams as

before. Neil Hodgson stayed with the INS/GSE team, with multiple-times champion Niall McKenzie taking Bayliss' place. In the Reve Red Bull Team, James Haydon joined stalwart rider John Reynolds. The season started brilliantly for Ducati, with Reynolds, Haydon and Hodgson dominating. Often there were three Ducatis on the podium. Although supplied by Ducati Corse, the British engines were prepared by their respective teams, still providing similar performance to the factory Infostrada machines. After a closely fought year, Hodgson ended the season winning his first British Superbike Championship.

The new pretender, Troy Bayliss, with the retiring master Fogarty. Bayliss took over from the injured Fogarty during 2000 and immediately impressed with some fine results.

2001

With the release of the new Testastretta 998cc engine and the limited edition 996 R at the end of 2000, a new 998cc World Superbike racer could be homologated for 2001. Already Luca Cadalora had tested a 'lab' version of the 998 during 2000. Although this engine had new crankcases and a shorter stroke, it still didn't feature the Testastretta cylinder heads. Even so, the results were promising, and, after a disappointing season in 2000, Ducati Corse had high hopes for 2001. The big news for 2001 was the retirement of Carl Fogarty. After disappointing tests at Mugello in September 2000, Fogarty finally announced his expected retirement. This left the door open for Troy Bayliss to succeed him..

Ducati Corse supported two teams in World Superbike. In the Team Ducati Infostrada, Ruben Xaus joined Bayliss, while Ben Bostrom resumed full works status, but in a separate L&M-sponsored team, on Dunlop tyres. Both teams were run under the direction of Tardozzi, and they were the only teams with the Testastretta engine for 2001. The 998cc 996R01 had a bore and stroke of 100 x 63.5mm and, with 42mm inlet valves and 34mm exhaust valves, a single injector Marelli IWF1 with 60mm throttle bodies, the new Testastretta produced a claimed 174bhp at 12,200rpm. The new engine was 3kg lighter than before, and the redesigned fairing with filled-in ducts improved the drag coefficient by one per cent. Chassis updates included external pressurisation chambers on the Öhlins 42mm front fork and a choice of three sizes of front brake disc.

Bayliss was immediately happier with the 998, and, with six wins, he took the Riders' Championship. After a slow start, Bostrom won five races in succession and Ducati

gained its tenth manufacturer's title, with 15 wins. At the final round at Imola, Bayliss fronted with a silver paint scheme replicating the Imola 200 Formula 750 racers of nearly 30 years earlier.

For 2001, the 996R01 gained a new fairing without side air scoops, aiding aerodynamics.

As was usual practice, the customer 996RS was similar to the previous year's factory bike, retaining the earlier 98 x 64mm 996cc Desmoquattro engine. With the shorter intake system of the 2000 factory racers, power was increased to 168 horsepower at 12,000rpm. The forks were 42mm Öhlins, with radial caliper Brembo front brakes. Hodgson proved surprisingly competitive against the new generation factory machines in the World

The heart of the 996R01 was the new Testastretta engine.

Troy Bayliss capably filled Fogarty's shoes and comfortably won the 2001 World Superbike Championship.

Ben Bostrom demonstrating the style that took him to five consecutive World Superbike race victories during 2001.

Superbike Championship, and, in Britain, John Reynolds, Sean Emmett, and Steve Hislop were unbeatable. Veterans Hislop and Reynolds fought for the Championship title all year, Reynolds eventually prevailing.

Ducati still wanted to win the elusive AMA Superbike Championship, and particularly the Daytona 200, although the high costs involved in AMA racing were still a burden. Unlike for World Superbike, sponsorship wasn't easy to obtain. In an effort to improve results, the racing effort in the US was in-house for the first time, with Ducati North America sponsoring two dealer racing teams. The Competition Accessories Team retained Larry Pegram, also signing John Kocinski.

Additionally, Hansen Motorcycles (HMC) of Manitowoc, Wisconsin, was chosen to receive factory support. Here, former World Superbike Champion and five-time Daytona 200 winner Scott Russell was given a one-year contract, alongside Steve Rapp, but Russell's season came to a premature end in a horrific start line crash at Daytona. Andreas Meklau was drafted to replace Russell, but he struggled with the circuits. Mitch Hansen's team was managed by Alister Wager and included former Fogarty mechanic, Anthony 'Slick' Bass. Despite the huge factory effort, results were not forthcoming. Ducati was absent from the rostrum all season, and this year was one to forget for Ducati North America.

World Superbike Championship victories 2001

Date	Location	Race	Winner
1 April	Kyalami, SA	Race 2	Ben Bostrom
13 May	Monza, Italy	Race 1 & 2	Troy Bayliss
27 May	Donington, GB	Race 1	Neil Hodgson
10 June	Lausitz, Germany	Race 2	Troy Bayliss
24 June	Misano, Italy	Race 1	Troy Bayliss
		Race 2	Ben Bostrom
8 July	Laguna Seca, USA	Race 1 & 2	Ben Bostrom
29 July	Brands Hatch, GB	Race 1 & 2	Ben Bostrom
3 September	Oschersleben, Germany	Race 2	Ruben Xaus
9 September	Assen, Holland	Race 1 & 2	Troy Bayliss
30 September	Imola, Italy	Race 1	Ruben Xaus

2002

Although the 998 was now an interim model until the advent of the new 999, Ducati Corse continued to update the Factory Superbike and this year it received a second generation Testastretta engine. Chief Engineer Filippo Preziosi enlarged the engine slightly to 999cc, with a 104mm bore and 58.8mm stroke. All the engine castings were new, as was the Magneti Marelli MF3S engine management system. The throttle bodies were non-cylindrical (still with a single injector per cylinder) and, with a revised exhaust system, the power of the 998F02 went up to 188bhp at 12,500rpm. Braking updates improvement saw metallic brake pads, allowing 290mm front discs to be used all season.

During the season, updates included the installation of a cooling duct from the right side of the radiator to the rear cambelt and pulley.

There were new minimum weight regulations for 2002. The 1000cc twin's weight was now 164kg, with the 750cc fours 159kg, a reversal of the original regulations that were drafted when fours were dominant. The change reflected the success of Ducati's process of continual evolution that had seen it continue to dominate the World Superbike Championship.

Bostrom's L&M-sponsored 998F02 ran Dunlop, rather than Michelin tyres, and Bostrom struggled all season.

The Testastretta engine was completely redesigned for 2002; this year was the last for the 916-inspired chassis.

World Superbike Championship victories 2002

10 March	Valencia, Spain	Race 1 & 2	Troy Bayliss
24 March	Phillip Island, Australia	Race 1 & 2	Troy Bayliss
7 April	Kyalami, SA	Race 1 & 2	Troy Bayliss
12 May	Monza, Italy	Race 1 & 2	Troy Bayliss
26 May	Silverstone, GB	Race 2	Troy Bayliss
9 June	Lausitz, Germany	Race 1 & 2	Troy Bayliss
23 June	Misano, Italy	Race 1 & 2	Troy Bayliss
14 July	Laguna Seca, USA	Race 1	Troy Bayliss

With no change to the official factory Superbike team line-up for 2002, Ducati narrowly failed in its quest for another World Superbike Championship. In one of the most exciting racing seasons ever, Bayliss set the stage with 14 victories, before Colin Edwards countered on the Honda SP-2 to win the final eight races, and the Championship by nine points. The HM Plant Team, with riders Hodgson and James Toseland, ran the 2001-spec 998F01s, with a claimed 179bhp at 12,000rpm, and weighing in at 165kg. The customer 998RS was a Testastretta this year, and was also competitive in the hands of Lucio Pedercini and Juan Borja.

Ducati was also back in force contesting the British and AMA Superbike Championships. Steve Hislop, riding for Paul Bird's MonsterMob, was equipped with a customer 998 Testastretta, as were the Renegade duo of Michael Rutter and Shane Byrne. In one of the most exciting seasons ever, the Ducatis totally dominated, Hislop winning the title. The season was, again, less satisfactory in the US. HMC was now the only sponsored team, and began the season at Daytona with Canadian rider Pascal Picotte. Political machinations saw Picotte fired, replaced by ex-Kawasaki veteran Superbike champion Doug Chandler. Chandler brought along tuner, Gary Medley, and immediately provided Ducati with improved results. It didn't win any races, but at least Chandler saw the podium three times, and finished eighth overall in the standings.

After a strong start, Bayliss slumped towards the end of the season, eventually narrowly losing the 2002 World Superbike Championship.

James Toseland showed there was still some life left in the older 998; easily winning the second World Superbike race at Oschersleben.

2003

While the official factory racers were now based on the new 999, the 2002 998 F02 bikes were run in World Superbike by the Colin Wright's GSE Team. Piloted by James Toseland and Chris Walker, Toseland won one race: Race 2 at Oschersleben. The 998F02 was identical to Bayliss' machine of the previous year, sharing the 104 x 58.8mm Testastretta engine with the factory 999F03. With single injector IWF1 throttle bodies controlled by a Magnetti Marelli processor, the 999cc engine produced 188 horsepower at 12,500rpm. Updated suspension included the newer pressurised 42mm Öhlins of the factory 999F03, and the claimed weight with ballast was 164kg. Unlike the factory bikes, GSE ran Dunlop tyres.

There were several private 998RS machines on the grid, along with Chili riding for PSG-1 Ducati and Laconi for NCR. The 998RS Testastretta was the earlier 100 x 63.5mm unit, producing around 175 horsepower at 12,000rpm. Chili won the first race at Laguna Seca, and Laconi regularly finished on the podium.

The Ducati 998 continued to dominate the British Superbike Championship, but this year it was Shane 'Shakey' Byrne who took the series on the MonsterMob Ducati, with 12 victories. Replacing Hislop, who was dumped by the team over the winter, Byrne had two new F02 Superbikes at his disposal, and also managed to surprise the World Superbike field at Brands Hatch as a wild card entry, with back-to-back victories. Michael Rutter, riding for the Renegade Team, had two well-used F02 bikes, but lacked the spares and backup to consistently battle at the front.

Ducati's woes in the AMA Championship continued during 2003. Two teams started the season: Ducati Austin with Anthony Gobert, and the Dream Team with Larry Pegram. While Gobert was sacked again mid-season, and replaced by Giovanni Bussei, the Dream Team quietly faded away altogether. At least Bussei made amends: finishing second in the final race.

World Superbike Championship victories (998) 2003

1 June	Oschersleben, Germany	Race 2	James Toseland
14 July	Laguna Seca, USA	Race 1	Pierfrancesco Chili
27 July	Brands Hatch, GB	Race 1 & 2	Shane Byrne

Shane Byrne dominated the 2003 British Superbike Championship on the MonsterMob 998F02.

The final years

2002 model year

For 2002, the 998cc Testastretta engine powered all the large displacement Superbikes, now with the generic title '998.' The 998 R replaced the 996 R, and was the only model to feature the short stroke 999cc motor, while the 748 range (still with the Desmoquattro engine) was unchanged but for colours. All fairings were the improved aerodynamic type of the previous 996 R, constructed in techo-polymer, except for the 998 R which retained a carbon-fibre fairing, with new fairing decals, specific to each model. Other updates to all 998s and 748s included new tailpiece graphics (also dependent on the model), new tailpiece decals with 'Ducati Superbike,' and a new tank decal featuring the Italian flag and 'No 1' encircled in a laurel wreath.

998 R

Heading the range was the spectacular 998 R. Powered by a second series Testastretta displacing 999cc, this retained the deep sump sandcast type crankcases, but incorporated many small engine improvements. Now with a 104mm bore and 58.8mm stroke, and a higher 12.3:1 compression ratio, power was increased to 139 horsepower at 10,000rpm, and torque to 10.7kgm at 8000rpm. To handle the extra power, the Testastretta crank output shaft now rode in twin ball bearings, instead of the single unit of the Desmoquattro. The 998 R intake valve diameter was unchanged from the 996 R at 40mm, as were the camshafts with 11.71mm lift, and the exhaust valve diameter also unchanged at

The 2002 998R continued the style initiated by the previous 996R.

Clockwise from top left: Powering the 998R was a short-stroke deep sump Testastretta engine; The 998R tailpiece featured a 'Ducati Corse' shield; The 998R tailpiece was without vents; Setting the 998R apart from the 996R were lighter Marchesini wheels and offset front disc rotors.

33mm, with 10.13mm lift. Since the valves were titanium, special valve seats and guides were required. As on the 996 R, the intake valves opened 16° before TDC, closing 60° after BDC, while the exhaust valves opened at 60° before BDC, closing 18° after TDC. The inclination of the intake and exhaust valves on the 998 R was also the same as the 996 R, at 12° and 13° respectively from the cylinder-head axis, providing an included valve angle of 25°. Another advantage of the Testastretta was improved breathing, and, as the intake ports were only tilted 35° (compared to 43° on the Desmoquattro), the reduced bend to the valve seats dramatically improving the mixture swirl. The ports were also larger, at 33mm (instead of 29mm) for the intake side, and 29mm (versus 27.5mm) on the exhaust. A tiny 10mm (as opposed to 12mm on the Desmoquattro) sparkplug ignited the mixture.

As on the 996 R Testastretta, the cam belts and idler sprocket sizes and locations were different from the 996 Desmoquattro. The belts were wider (21mm as opposed to 17mm), with more teeth per inch and fitted to new adjustable 20-tooth cam sprockets (versus 18mm on the Desmoquattro). The idler pulleys were also larger (48mm diameter compared to 39.5mm), minimising the pressure angle on the belts, and were placed closer to the centres of the long runs, reducing belt slap and resulting in more precise valve timing. The water pump was also new, with a larger 60mm impeller (as opposed to 54mm) providing 15% more flow. The more-compact Testastretta engine was 2kg lighter than the Desmoquattro. The fuel-injection system was the same Marelli 5.9 M as the 2001 996 R, with 54mm throttle bodies and a single 'shower-head'-style injector standing above the air intake. The shower-head injector sprayed in a tight 15° pattern straight down the port, whereas the angle-mounted twin-injectors of the 996 used a 30° pattern, to avoid squirting so much fuel directly onto the port walls, where it caused fuel sheeting. Raw fuel running off the port walls was unlikely to achieve full combustion, but fuel that remained atomised burned more rapidly. Also shared with the 996 R was a larger airbox and lighter throttle position sensors.

Chassis updates included a carbon-fibre seat (without air intakes), and a 'Ducati Corse' shield, 4.5mm offset front brake discs with new Brembo four-piston four-pad calipers, lighter Marchesini wheels (-400g front, and -800g rear), and Öhlins suspension. The front fork featured TiN-coated fork tubes to reduce friction, the rear view mirrors now matched the fairing colour, and the frame was the racing type of the 996 R. As the final example of the 916-derived limited edition homologation models, the 998 R was possibly the finest. While the later 999R was arguably an improved motorcycle, the 998 R best combined timeless 916 style with the newer generation Testastretta engine.

998 S

The previous 996 R Testastretta engine now powered the 998 S; this retaining the 998cc dimensions of 100 x 63.5mm, 11.4:1 compression ratio and deep sump sandcast crankcase. Other than the bore and stroke, and compression ratio, the engine specifications were similar to the 998 R, with the same valves and camshafts, Marelli 5.9 injection with single shower-type injector, 54mm throttle bodies and larger capacity airbox. The power of 136 horsepower at 10,000rpm, and torque of 10.31kgm at 8000rpm, was also the same as the 996 R. However, the 998 S chassis specification was lower than the 996 R and 998 R, now including an adjustable Showa front fork (with TiN-coated tubes), instead of Öhlins, but with racing type frame and Öhlins

The 998S production line, with Troy Bayliss' 998 F02 World Superbike racer in the foreground.

The 998S's deep sump 998cc Testastretta was carried over from the 996R.

The 998S was also available as a Biposto. Colour was either red or yellow.

rear shock absorber. Available in Monoposto and Biposto, other higher specification components on the 998 S included a carbon-fibre fairing belly pan and Öhlins steering damper. The braking system also featured thinner (4.5mm) front brake discs, new style four-pad Brembo brake calipers and the 996 R and 748 R's 15mm front master cylinder (down from 16mm) to reduce front lever pressure. For the United States, the higher horsepower 998cc Testastretta wasn't street legal, so US 998 Ss included the lower (123) horsepower 998 engine, but featured the 998 R Öhlins front fork.

998

Replacing the 996 for 2002, the base 998 included a high sump crankcase Testastretta. Compared to the 998 R and 998 S, the 998 combustion chambers and crankcases were high-accuracy die-castings instead of machined sand-casting; the crankcases a high sump design. As on the 998 R and 998 S, valve sizes were 40mm and 33mm, but new camshafts were considerably milder, the inlet opening 4° before TDC, closing 56° after BDC, while the exhaust valves opened at 53° before BDC, closing 11° after TDC. Valve lift was 10.15mm for the inlet and 9.1mm for the exhausts. To improve reliability, the 998's cams had less aggressive opening and closing ramps than the 996 Desmoquattro it replaced, but with higher lift. The reduced overlap also improved fuel economy while reducing emissions. As the Testastretta was envisaged to work at higher rpm than the Desmoquattro, the 100mm pistons were lighter, with redesigned piston rings. Following computer simulation, and Ferrari Formula One experience, that predicted piston rocking in the bore would cause ring flutter and compromise sealing, the 998's top ring was now thinner (1mm as opposed to

1.5mm), and made of steel instead of cast iron. The profile was angled in a cone shape, and the edge barrel-faced. Under compression and combustion pressure, the ring flattened out, but returned to its cocked position when the exhaust valve opened. The second ring was also slightly thinner than on the 996 Desmoquattro, at 1mm (versus 1.2mm).

The 998 shared a number of components with the 998 R and 998 S, too, this including the Marelli 5.9 injection system, 54mm throttle bodies, single 'shower-head' injector and larger airbox. Other new features included lighter throttle position sensors and ultrasonically welded plastic air intake tubes (instead of the 996's aluminium). The Marelli 5.9 EFI had

The base 998 Testastretta had pressure-diecast cylinder heads and crankcases.

Opposite top: A cutaway of the yellow Monoposto 998
bodywork; bottom: The 998 featured the earlier two-pad
Brembo brake calipers.

more than twice the mapping points of the 996's Marelli 1.6 system, was one-quarter the size and faster, at 20Mhz as opposed to the 1.6's 16Mhz. With a 45mm exhaust system and aluminium Termignoni mufflers, power was 123 horsepower at 9750rpm, with torque of 9.89kgm at 8000rpm.

The 998 chassis was essentially that of the 998 S, with the metallic grey racing frame, five-spoke Marchesini wheels, Showa front fork (with TiN-coated tubes), and Öhlins rear suspension; while the front brakes included the previous 996 R's 4.5mm discs – although the four-piston Brembo brake calipers were still the two-pad type. As with the 998 S, the 998 was available as a Biposto or Monoposto.

The 998 crankcases differed from the 998S and 998R, as
the sump was shallower.

998 S Bayliss, 998 S Bostrom

Later in 2001, Ducati announced two limited edition 998 Ss: the Bayliss 998 S, and Bostrom 998 S. Both included an Öhlins front fork and special graphics (plus number plate and signature), but were otherwise identical to the regular 998 S. While not as special as the

short-stroke 998 R, 300 998 S Bayliss sold in less than two days, when it was released on the internet. US versions had the 123-horsepower 998 engine, and more carbon-fibre bodywork, to compensate for the lower power. The Bostrom 998 S was similar to the Bayliss, with three series of 155 produced; one for the US (with the 123 horsepower motor), another 155 for the rest of the world, and 155 for Europe. (Both these series had the 136 horsepower motor).

The limited edition Bayliss 998S carried the livery of the 2001 World Superbike racer.

Unlike the standard 998S, the 998S Bayliss included an Öhlins front fork.

Another 998S limited edition was the Bostrom, decked out in the garish L&M sponsorship colour scheme.

748 R, 748 S, 748

Apart from Titanium Grey with red wheels offered on the 748 S, all three 748s were largely unchanged for 2002. All featured the 998's new smooth fairing and fairing decals, 'Ducati Superbike' tailpiece decals, and new Italian flag and laurel wreath tank decal. Rear view mirrors also matched the fairing, this year. The unchanged 748 Desmoquattro engine produced 97 horsepower at 11,000rpm and torque of 7.4kgm at 9000rpm on the basic and S versions, and 106 horsepower at 11,500rpm and torque of 7.6kgm at 9000rpm on the R version. The chassis was also unchanged from 2001, the R version featuring a chrome-molybdenum frame (with thinner walls compared to the rest of the Superbike range), as used in Supersport Championship racing. All 748s were equipped with a fully adjustable front fork (Showa on the basic version and S; Öhlins on the R), with TiN-coated tubes on the

S and R versions. The rear suspension was an adjustable Sachs rear shock absorber on the basic version, Showa on the S, and Öhlins on the R. The 748 R also received the four-pad Brembo front brake calipers, and the 'Ducati Corse' shield on the tailpiece as on the 998 R. The 748 range mirrored the 998, as both the basic and S versions were available as Monoposto or Biposto.

The 748R was largely unchanged for 2002, retaining the 106 horsepower Desmoquattro engine. The front brakes included Brembo four-pad calipers.

Along with new graphics and a smooth fairing, the 748S was available in this striking Titanium grey with red wheels for 2002.

The 748S wheels were five-spoke Marchesini.

All 2002 748s had this celebratory tank decal.

Monster S4 Fogarty, Monster S4

In honour of Carl Fogarty, its most successful ever racer, Ducati offered, in June 2001, a limited edition Monster S4 Fogarty, for sale over the internet. Essentially a standard 916cc Monster S4, there were a number of updates to justify the €18,000 price. This was driven, in October 2000, by Daniele Casolari of Ducati Performance. Casolari asked the stylist Aldo Drudi to create new colour-coded bodywork, along with reshaping the fuel tank and incorporating additional carbon fibre body parts. The Foggy S4 received upgraded Showa 43mm forks with TiN-coated fork legs. The weight was reduced to 189kg. The optional high level exhaust system with oval carbon

fibre Termignoni mufflers saw the power climb to 110 horsepower at 9750rpm. 142 of the 300 Fogarty S4s offered were sold within the first 24 hours of their release over the internet on June 20, 2001. Each bike came with an exclusive Poggipolini-etched titanium plate, with Foggy logo, his signature, and the bike's serial number.

As it had only been released a year earlier, the Monster S4 for 2002 was little changed. All Desmoquattro engines received new cambelt tensioner hubs, and an oil jet to the vertical piston in the left crankcase. Other detail updates were a safety lockout system (incorporated in the CPU) to control the sidestand, clutch and gearbox, and a new fairing mount. The colours of red, yellow, black, or metallic dark grey were unchanged.

The engine in the Fogarty Monster S4 was still the 916cc Desmoquattro of the standard Monster S4.

A Fogarty Monster S4 at the Ducati factory, underneath
a Fogarty mural, in late 2001.

As on the Monster S4, little attempt was made to beautify the Fogarty S4's engine's appearance, with the water pump still prominent on the left.

The 2002 Monster S4 in black.

Sport Touring colours were unchanged for 2002: the ST4 was still available in yellow.

ST4, ST4S

Updates to the ST4 and ST4S for 2002 were minor, including only a silencer with a Euro 2 standard compliant catalytic converter (except for the US), and an aluminium clutch housing and discs replacing the steel of 2001. The engine and chassis were unchanged, the ST4S retaining a fully adjustable Öhlins monoshock with remote pre-load adjustment, aluminium swingarm and five-spoke Marchesini wheels, shod with hyper-sport tires (Pirelli Dragon Evo, Michelin Pilot Sport, or Dunlop D204). The ST4S featured 5mm-thick front brake discs (versus the 4mm of the discs of the ST4), which were less susceptible to overheating. For 2002, the frame and wheels were metallic dark grey, and the engine metallic silver grey.

Right: The ST4S from above: with standard luggage this was an extremely effective and comfortable sport touring motorcycle.

The ST4S unclothed: the engine was the 996 Desmoquattro, and the wheels and suspension higher specification than the ST4.

The 996 as used in the film *The Matrix: Reloaded.* Ducati brought out a limited edition in the same dark green, but as production of the 996 had ceased, this was a 998.

2003 model year

Although, for 2003, the 999 and 749 replaced the 998 and 748, respectively, as Ducati's primary Superbikes, the 998 and 748 were still available this year, as a standard version only (in red or yellow with a metallic grey frame and wheels). The Sport Touring family expanded to include the ST4's ABS with anti-lock braking. All 2003 Model year examples had a redesigned and improved gear selector drum, improving shifting action and eliminating false neutrals, and an external 12 volt outlet that also allows battery recharging. The ST4S and ST4S ABS also had a new starter safety system. Up to model year 2002, the starter safety system did not allow the engine to run with the sidestand down, preventing the rider from starting out with it in that position. This was designed to increase safety, but the engine could not be warmed up while on its sidestand. The new system allowed the engine to run with the stand lowered and the bike in neutral. Instead, the safety system now stopped the engine as soon as the clutch lever was pulled if the stand was down, making it impossible to ride away.

ST4's ABS

The ST4's ABS was the first Ducati to include an Anti Lock Braking System (ABS). This system had been produced by Bosch, with the settings developed by Brembo in collaboration with Ducati. The system utilised a control unit that, by means of valves and pumps, managed the pressure in the braking circuits of the front and rear brake calipers. The input signals to the control unit depended on the actuation of the rider's controls (front brake lever and rear brake pedal), and by wheel speed sensors. When the sensors deteced a wheel slowing too

much in relation to the calculated speed of the motorcycle, a valve reduced the pressure in the circuit, preventing wheel lock-up. The control unit allowed 90% utilisation of the available grip, making efficient braking possible even in cases of panic stopping, or when surfaces offer inadequate grip. The ABS braking system adopted by Ducati also allowed separate ABS management of the two braking systems, front and rear. The ST4's ABS came in new metallic grey with red wheels and new graphics, the side vents and filler plug colour matched to the fairing, or silver on the dark metallic grey model.

Apart from new pick-up coils (now held by one bolt in the left engine cover), there were no changes to the Monster S4. After only three years, the S4 was about to be replaced by the S4R, released during 2003 as an early model year 2004 example. In May 2003, Ducati announced the 998 Matrix, in the same dark green as the 996 Superbike used in the film *The Matrix: Reloaded,* the first of two sequels to the highly successful *The Matrix*. This film featured a dramatic road chase on a Ducati.

ABS was available on the ST4s for 2003: metallic grey with red wheels.

2004 model year

By 2004, the 999 and 749 range was firmly established. Two final versions of the 998 were released: the 998S FE (Final Edition), and 998 Matrix. The 998S FE was similar to the earlier 998S, with an Öhlins front fork, Biposto or Monoposto, while the 998 Matrix was a 998, painted dark green like the one in the film. The ST4 was discontinued, with the ST4S and ST4S ABS the only four-valve Sport Touring models available during this year. The 996cc Monster S4R also replaced the 916cc Monster S4.

Monster S4R

The S4R was released in April 2003 as an early 2004 model, 'R' indicating Racing. This was the first product to appear under the auspices of new Monster Project Leader Giulio Malagoli, and the S4R combined features of a few existing models to create a distinctive and high performing naked motorcycle. Powering the S4 Monster was the 996cc liquid-cooled four-valve Desmoquattro engine of the ST4S. With a bore and stroke of 96 x 68.8mm (according to the 2004 press release), or 94 x 66mm (from the Owners' Manual), but more likely unchanged in bore and stroke from the ST4S and 996, the engine displaced 996cc and had an 11.6:1 compression ratio. The distinctive dropped exhaust camshaft cylinder head format of the 916cc S4 allowed a further forward engine position. Further contributing to the excellent weight distribution was a curved oil radiator beneath the similarly shaped radiator. To improve the visual aspect of the water-cooled Desmoquattro, the timing belt covers were carbon-fibre. The six-speed gearbox was new, with a sportier shift action due to a shorter lever throw, and wider ratios than the S4. Bottom was shorter, and the two top gears longer, allowing a top speed in the vicinity of 255km/h. Although the Desmoquattro engine had been in production for 16 years, it still suffered from minor problems, particularly valve rocker arm damage. In mid-2004

The Matrix Limited Edition 998 was available in 2003 and 2004. Aside from the colour, this was a standard 998.

Ducati released a new 4th generation rocker arm without the copper layer under the chrome (as on the two-valve engines). The electronic fuel-injection was the Marelli 5.9 system with 50mm throttle bodies, and a new high level two-one-two exhaust system with aluminium muffler covers exited on the right. This Euro 2-friendly exhaust contributed to a power output of 113 horsepower at 8750rpm, with maximum torque of 9.68kgm at 7000rpm (12 horsepower and 0.38kgm up on the S4).

Unlike some other high-performance naked motorcycles that were essentially Superbikes stripped of a fairing (such as Aprilia's Tuono), the S4R was still ostensibly a Monster with a more powerful engine. The Brembo-built steel frame was similar to the S4 (still based on the ST4 sport tourer), but with a new lighter steering head, and 4.3kg tubular aluminium single-sided swingarm derived from the limited edition MH900ie (Mike Hailwood Evoluzione). The suspension included a fully adjustable 43mm upside down Showa fork with TiN-coated tubes, and an adjustable Showa shock absorber. Ride height adjustment was obtainable separate from spring preload, and the riding position and controls were updated, with Magura aluminium variable section handlebars, and four-way adjustable brake and clutch levers.

The Brembo brakes and five-spoke Marchesini wheels were carried over from the S4, with a pair of 320 x 5mm front discs, 30/34-4 pistons calipers and a PS16 master cylinder. The rear 245mm disc was 1mm thicker (at 6mm), to improve heat dissipation.

The 996cc ST4's engine powered the 2004 Monster S4R, and it was the highest performing Monster yet.

With 113 horsepower powering a moderate 193kg, the S4R was a formidable performance motorcycle, the new swingarm and exhaust system successfully rejuvenating the decade-old design.

ST4S, ST4S ABS

For 2004, the ST4S was stylistically updated with a new front fairing: taller than before, with a new headlight.Remote light beam height adjustment, electronically controlled from the instrument panel, allowed adjustment for varying loads. Also new was a fully electronic

instrument panel, with modern graphics, and height adjustable handlebars. A new seat shape and padding improved comfort. The CAN line electronic system was new, too; first introduced on the Ducati 999 series, this simplifed and lightened the electrical system and wire harness. Apart from the fairing and seat, the ST4S chassis was unchanged this year.

The Monster S4R's distinctive double muffler arrangement.

The Monster S4R had a single-sided aluminium swingarm, too.

The ST series received a new fairing and headlight for 2004.

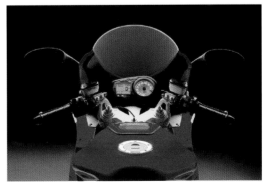

Also new was the dashboard and electronic display.

2005 model year

By 2005, Tamburini's iconic 916 Superbike and its derivatives had finished, finally replaced by the controversial 999. Ironically, just as the 916 was consigned to history, plans were afoot for a 916-inspired 999 replacement: the 1098. This would appear in 2007. In the meantime, Massimo Bordi's venerable Desmoquattro soldiered on in the ST4S, ST4S ABS, and Monster S4R.

ST4S, ST4S ABS

As it was significantly updated for 2004, the ST4S and ST4S ABS were little changed for 2005. To reduce the time required for scheduled maintenance, the fairing fasteners were updated, and an oil bath clutch, with new dampers, was introduced to reduce noise and improve the gearshift. The claimed power was now 121 Horsepower at 8750rpm, with torque of 10.5kgm at 7250rpm. This would be the final year for the four-valve ST4.

After only two years with the new fairing, the ST4S ceased production in 2005.

Monster S4R

Although the style of the S4R was unchanged for 2005, the Desmoquattro engine (according to the 2005 press release) bore and stroke was now 98 x 66mm (still providing 996cc), but it was probably the same as the previous year. The claimed power increased to

117 horsepower at 8750rpm with 10.1kgm of torque at 7000rpm. The frame, suspension, and brakes were largely unchanged from 2004, but the rear disc was now a 245 x 5mm. 2005 models were available not only in classic single colour black, but in blue with a white stripe, too, and also in two new colours: Ducati red, and black – both with white stripes.

The Monster S4R was available in red with a white stripe for 2005.

2006 model year

With the demise of the ST4S, only the Monster S4R and new S4RS were left as remnants of the era that began with the 916. The Testastretta-powered S4RS was the most powerful Monster yet – now upstaged at the head of the Monster line-up, the S4R continued unchanged for 2006. It was the only model with the venerable Desmoquattro engine that remained in Ducati's line-up: this would be its final year before it, too, succumbed to the Testastretta.

Monster S4RS Testastretta

With increasing demand for a blend between naked styling and new-generation power, it was inevitable that the Testastretta engine would appear in the Monster range sooner rather than later, and the first example was the S4RS. Powering the S4RS was a deep sump 998cc Testastretta (as on the 998 and 999 S), with a 100 x 63.5mm bore and stroke, 11.4:1 compression ratio, and 40mm and 33mm valves. On the S4RS, a special, larger, triangular-shaped oil cooler sat underneath the front cylinder, and the overall engine weight of 71kg was 3kg less than the Desmoquattro, altering the weight bias slightly to 49/51 (from 50/50 on the S4R).

A new Marelli 5AM ECU controlled a single external 12-hole IWP 189 injector into a 50mm throttle body (compared to 54mm on the 999), while the exhaust headers and collectors were increased to 45mm (up from the S4R's 40mm). With a catalytic converter in a large collector underneath, the S4RS met Euro 3 emissions. Twin Termignoni aluminium mufflers were stacked on the right. The resulting engine provided slightly less power than the 999, but still an impressive 130 horsepower at 9500rpm (or 119 horsepower at 9250rpm according to the Owners' Manual), with a maximum torque of 10.6kgm at 7500rpm.

Housing the powerful Testastretta engine was an updated version of the Brembo-built S4R tubular steel trellis frame. Detail changes around the airbox resulted in a 5% increase in torsional rigidity. The black-painted tubular aluminium single-sided swingarm was from the S4R, while the wheels, suspension and brakes were all considerably upgraded. The 5.5in rear Marchesini Y-spoked wheel was 23% lighter than that of the S4R, providing an 18% reduction in inertia. The brakes and suspension were by far the highest specification ever to grace a Monster. The 43mm fully adjustable Öhlins front fork low friction TiN treated sliders came off the 999 S, as did the radial mounted four-piston front P4.34B brake calipers with 320mm discs (5mm thick) on aluminium carriers. Completing the impressive braking system was a radial PR 18/19 master cylinder, while the rear brake was a 245 x 5mm disc with a Brembo P32F caliper and PS 11B master cylinder.

Sharp steering was obtained by a 30mm offset in the triple clamps. The top triple clamp also included a 45mm cast riser for the variable section tapered aluminium Magura handlebar. To complement the naked look, and improve the aesthetics of the liquid-cooled engine, a number of carbon-fibre components were included, notably the front mudguard, timing belt covers and the exhaust pipe heat shield. Although the dimensions were unchanged from the S4R, the weight was reduced to 177kg, providing the S4RS with a class-leading power-to-weight ratio.

The Monster S4RS had Superbike specification suspension, wheels and brakes. Also setting the Monster S4RS apart was the deep sump Testastretta engine.

2007 model year and beyond

After 21 years, the venerable Desmoquattro engine in its last incarnation finally surrendered to the Testastretta. Just as the 998 had eclipsed the 996 in the Superbike family, so it finally did with the founder of the Monster SR family, the S4R. The Monster S4RS continued largely unchanged this year, but, under new ownership, Ducati was changing rapidly, and it was only a matter of time before all remnants of the 916 era finally disappeared.

Monster S4R Testastretta, S4RS Tricolore

For 2007, the S4R received the deep sump 998cc 130 horsepower engine of the S4RS, only chassis specification now separating the two leading models of the Monster family. The chassis continued with an adjustable 43mm Showa upside-down fork and adjustable Sachs remote reservoir shock. An adjustable pushrod enabled ride-height setting independent of spring pre-load. Radially mounted Brembo front brake calipers provided state-of-art stopping, and all versions had a red painted frame with black swingarm and matching lower front fork. The black colour scheme continued with headlamp mounts, fork clamps, handlebar risers, footrests and radiator side covers.

The Monster range was revamped after 2007, with the existing models gradually discontinued. The range-leading S4RS Testastretta was available in 2008 as a Special Edition Tricolore, a feature used by Ducati in the past to extend the life of models about to be terminated. This combined the Tricolore colour scheme of the tank, tailpiece and headlamp

The Monster S4RS's 130 horsepower Testastretta engine powered the Monster S4R for 2007.

fairing with a gold-painted Trellis frame and Y-spoke wheels. Although the Monster S4R and S4RS continued to be available in 2009, these were unsold 2008 models.

By 2010, Ducati had moved into a new era for the Superbike and Monster, with the Multistrada replacing the Sport Touring. All links with the 916 were expunged. But, as the original 916 approaches its 25th birthday, its

The final traditional four-valve Monster was the 2008
S4RS Tricolore.

true value as a landmark motorcycle is finally
being appreciated. Today, the 916 is viewed
not only as one of Ducati's most significant
models, but also one of the most influential
modern motorcycle designs. The 916 set a new
aesthetic and functional blueprint for sporting
motorcycles, and was a ground breaking
design.

Appendix 1

Production 916/996/748 Technical Specifications 1994-2001

Model	916 Strada	916 SP	916 Biposto	916 Senna	916 Racing	748 Strada	748 Biposto	748 SP	916 Racing
Year	1994	1994-96	1995-98	1995-98	1995	1995-	1995-	1995-97	1996
Bore (mm)	94	94	94	94	96	88	88	88	96
Stroke (mm)	66	66	66	66	66	61.5	61.5	61.5	66
Capacity (cc)	916	916	916	916	955	748	748	748	955
Compression ratio	11:1	11.2:1	11:1	11:1	12:1	11.5:1	11.5:1	11.6:1	11.8:1
Max power (crank)	109bhp	131bhp	109bhp	109bhp	155bhp	98bhp	98bhp	104bhp	153bhp
Max rpm	10,000	11,500	10,000	10,000		11,500	11,500	11,500	
Valve timing inlet (1mm)	11° BTDC 70° ABDC	53° BTDC 71° ABDC	11° BTDC 70° ABDC	11° BTDC 70° ABDC	31° BTDC 78° ABDC	11° BTDC 70° ABDC	11° BTDC 70° ABDC	44° BTDC 72° ABDC	36° BTDC 72° ABDC
Valve timing exhaust (1mm)	62° BBDC 18° ATDC	77° BBDC 42° ATDC	62° BBDC 18° ATDC	62° BBDC 18° ATDC	71° BBDC 45° ATDC	62° BBDC 18° ATDC	62° BBDC 18° ATDC	77° BBDC 42° ATDC	71° BBDC 45° ATDC
Valve lift intake (mm)	9.60	11.0	9.60	9.60	12.0	9.60	9.60	10.85	12.0
Valve lift exh (mm)	8.74	9.0	8.74	8.74	10.5	8.74	8.74	9.0	10.5
EFI	P8	P8	1.6M	1.6M	P8	1.6M	1.6M	1.6M	P8
Front tyre	120/70ZR17	120/70ZR17	120/70ZR17	120/70ZR17	12/60 17SC	120/60ZR17	120/60ZR17	120/60ZR17	12/60 17SC
Rear tyre	190/50ZR17	190/50ZR17	190/50ZR17	190/50ZR17	18/76 17SC	180/55ZR17	180/55ZR17	180/55ZR17	18/76 17SC
Front brake	320mm Twin disc	320mm Twin disc	320mm Twin disc	320mm Twin disc	320mm Twin disc	320mm Twin disc	320mm Twin disc	320mm Twin disc	320mm Twin disc
Rear brake	220mm disc	220mm disc	220mm disc	220mm disc	200mm disc	220mm disc	220mm disc	220mm disc	200mm disc
Wheelbase	1410mm	1410mm	1410mm	1410mm	1420mm	1410mm	1410mm	1410mm	1420mm
Seat height	790mm	790mm	790mm	790mm	790mm	790mm	790mm	790mm	790mm
Length	2050mm	2050mm	2050mm	2050mm	2050mm	2050mm	2050mm	2050mm	2050mm
Width	685mm	685mm	685mm	685mm	685mm	685mm	685mm	685mm	685mm
Weight	198kg	192kg	204kg	198kg	154kg	200kg	202kg	198kg	160kg

Model	916 SPS	916 Racing	916 Racing	748 SPS	748 Racing	ST4	996	996 S	996 SPS
Year	1997-98	1997	1998	1998-99	1998-99	1999	1999-	1999-2000	1999
Bore (mm)	98	98	98	88	88	94	98	98	98
Stroke (mm)	66	66	66	61.5	61.5	66	66	66	66
Capacity (cc)	996	996	996	748	748	916	996	996	996
Compression ratio	11.5:1	12:1	12:1	11.6:1	11.6:1	11:1	11.5:1	11.5:1	11.5:1
Max power (crank)	123bhp	155bhp	151bhp	104bhp	108bhp	107bhp	112bhp	112bhp	123bhp
Max rpm	11,000			11,500	11,500	10,000	10,000	10,000	11,000
Valve timing inlet (1mm)	14° BTDC 73° ABDC	36° BTDC 72° ABDC	36° BTDC 72° ABDC	44° BTDC 72° ABDC	44° BTDC 72° ABDC	11° BTDC 70° ABDC	11° BTDC 70° ABDC	11° BTDC 70° ABDC	14° BTDC 73° ABDC
Valve timing exhaust (1mm)	57° BBDC 23° ATDC	69° BBDC 47° ATDC	69° BBDC 47° ATDC	77° BBDC 42° ATDC	77° BBDC 42° ATDC	62° BBDC 18° ATDC	62° BBDC 18° ATDC	62° BBDC 18° ATDC	57° BBDC 23° ATDC
Valve lift intake (mm)	10.8	12.0	12.0	10.85	10.85	9.60	9.60	9.60	10.8
Valve lift exh (mm)	9.8	10.5	10.5	9.0	9.0	8.74	8.74	8.74	9.8
EFI	P8	P8	P8	1.6M	1.6M	1.6M	1.6M	1.6M	P8
Front tyre	120/70ZR17	12/60 17SC	12/60 17SC	120/60ZR17	120/60ZR17	120/70ZR17	120/70ZR17	120/70ZR17	120/70ZR17
Rear tyre	190/50ZR17	18/76 17SC	18/60 17SC	180/55ZR17	180/55ZR17	170/60ZR17	190/50ZR17	190/50ZR17	190/50ZR17
Front brake	320mm Twin disc	320mm Twin disc	320mm Twin disc	320mm Twin disc	320mm Twin disc	320mm Twin disc	320mm Twin disc	320mm Twin disc	320mm Twin disc
Rear brake	220mm disc	200mm disc	200mm disc	220mm disc	220mm disc	245mm disc	220mm disc	220mm disc	220mm disc
Wheelbase	1410mm	1420mm	1430mm	1410mm	1410mm	1430mm	1410mm	1410mm	1410mm
Seat height	790mm	790mm	790mm	790mm	790mm	820mm	790mm	790mm	790mm
Length	2030mm	2050mm	2030mm	2030mm	2030mm	2070mm	2030mm	2030mm	2030mm
Width	780mm	685mm	685mm	780mm	685mm	910mm	780mm	780mm	780mm
Weight	190kg	162kg	155kg	194kg	170kg	212kg	198kg	190kg	190kg

Model	ST4	748 R	748 S	996 SPS	748 RS	Monster S4	ST4S	996 S	996 R
Year	2000-03	2000-02	2000-02	2000	2000-02	2001-03	2001-05	2001	2001
Bore (mm)	94	88	88	98	88	94	98	98	100
Stroke (mm)	66	61.5	61.5	66	61.5	66	66	66	63.5
Capacity (cc)	916	748	748	996	748	916	996	996	998
Compression ratio	11:1	11.5:1	11.5:1	11.5:1	12:1	11:1	11.5:1	11.5:1	11.4:1
Max power (crank)	105bhp	106bhp	97bhp	123bhp	124bhp	101bhp	117bhp	123bhp	135bhp
Max rpm	10,000	11,500	11,500	11,000	12,000	10,000	10,000	11,000	11,500
Valve timing Inlet (1mm)	11° BTDC 70° ABDC	20° BTDC 60° ABDC	11° BTDC 70° ABDC	14° BTDC 73° ABDC	30° BTDC 58° ABDC	11° BTDC 70° ABDC	11° BTDC 70° ABDC	14° BTDC 73° ABDC	16° BTDC 60° ABDC (0mm)
Valve timing Exhaust (1mm)	62° BBDC 18° ATDC	62° BBDC 38° ATDC	62° BBDC 18° ATDC	57° BBDC 23° ATDC	74° BBDC 38° ATDC	62° BBDC 18° ATDC	62° BBDC 18° ATDC	57° BBDC 23° ATDC	60° BBDC 18° ATDC (0mm)
Valve lift intake (mm)	9.60	12.5	9.60	10.8	12.5	9.60	9.60	10.8	11.71
Valve lift exh (mm)	8.74	10.5	8.74	9.8	10.5	8.74	8.74	9.8	10.13
EFI	1.6M	1.6M	1.6M	P8	1.6M	5.9M	5.9M	1.6M	5.9M
Front tyre	120/70ZR17	120/60ZR17	120/60ZR17	120/70ZR17	120/60ZR17	120/70ZR17 (120/65ZR17)	120/70ZR17	120/70ZR17	120/70ZR17
Rear tyre	180/55ZR17	180/55ZR17	180/55ZR17	190/50ZR17	180/55ZR17	180/55ZR17 (190/50ZR17)	180/55ZR17	190/50ZR17	190/50ZR17
Front brake	320mm Twin disc	320mm Twin disc	320mm Twin disc	320mm Twin disc	320mm Twin disc	320mm Twin disc	320mm Twin disc	320mm Twin disc	320mm Twin disc
Rear brake	245mm disc	220mm disc	220mm disc	220mm disc	220mm disc	245mm disc	245mm disc	220mm disc	220mm disc
Wheelbase	1430mm	1410mm	1410mm	1410mm	1415mm	1440mm	1430mm	1410mm	1410mm
Seat height	820mm	790mm	790mm	790mm	830mm	803mm	820mm	790mm	790mm
Length	2070mm	2030mm	2030mm	2030mm	2035mm	2070mm	2070mm	2030mm	2030mm
Width	910mm	780mm	780mm	780mm	680mm	775mm	910mm	780mm	780mm
Weight	215kg	192kg	196kg	187kg	172kg	190kg	212kg	198kg	185kg

Model	998	998 S	998 R	ST4s ABS	Monster S4R	Monster S4R	Monster S4RS	Monster S4R
Year	2002-04	2002-04	2002	2003-05	2003-04	2005-06	2006-07	2007
Bore (mm)	100	100	104	98	98	98	100	100
Stroke (mm)	63.5	63.5	58.8	66	66	66	63.5	63.5
Capacity (cc)	998	998	999	996	996	996	998	998
Compression ratio	11.4:1	11.4:1	12.3:1	11.5:1	11.6:1	11.2:1	11.4:1	11.4:1
Max power (crank)	123bhp	135bhp	139bhp	117bhp	113bhp	117bhp	130bhp	130bhp
Max rpm	11,500	11,500	11,500	10,000	10,000	10,000	11,000	11,000
Valve timing Inlet (1mm)	4° BTDC 56° ABDC (0mm)	16° BTDC 60° ABDC (0mm)	16° BTDC 60° ABDC (0mm)	11° BTDC 70° ABDC	11° BTDC 70° ABDC	11° BTDC 70° ABDC	16° BTDC 60° ABDC (0mm)	16° BTDC 60° ABDC (0mm)
Valve timing Exhaust (1mm)	53° BBDC 11° ATDC (0mm)	60° BBDC 18° ATDC (0mm)	60° BBDC 18° ATDC (0mm)	62° BBDC 18° ATDC	62° BBDC 18° ATDC	62° BBDC 18° ATDC	60° BBDC 18° ATDC (0mm)	60° BBDC 18° ATDC (0mm)
Valve lift intake (mm)	10.15	11.71	11.71	9.60	9.60	9.60	11.71	11.71
Valve lift exh (mm)	9.1	10.13	10.13	8.74	8.74	8.74	10.13	10.13
EFI	5.9M	5.9M	5.9M	5.9M	5.9M	5.9M	5AM	5AM
Front tyre	120/70ZR17	120/70ZR17	120/70ZR17	120/70ZR17	120/70ZR17	120/70ZR17	120/70ZR17	120/70ZR17
Rear tyre	190/50ZR17	190/50ZR17	190/50ZR17	180/55ZR17	180/55ZR17	180/55ZR17	180/55ZR17	180/55ZR17
Front brake	320mm Twin disc	320mm Twin disc	320mm Twin disc	320mm Twin disc	320mm Twin disc	320mm Twin disc	320mm Twin disc	320mm Twin disc
Rear brake	220mm disc	220mm disc	220mm disc	245mm disc	245mm disc	245mm disc	245mm disc	245mm disc
Wheelbase	1410mm	1410mm	1410mm	1430mm	1440mm	1440mm	1440mm	1440mm
Seat height	790mm	790mm	790mm	820mm	806mm	806mm	806mm	806mm
Length	2030	2030	2030	2070mm	2121mm	2121mm	2121mm	2121mm
Width	685	780	780	910mm	790mm	790mm	790mm	790mm
Weight	198kg	187kg	183kg	217kg	193kg	181kg	177kg	177kg

Appendix 2

Production Figures 748/916/996/ST4/Monster S4 1993-2001

748

Description	1994	1995	1996	1997	1998	1999	2000	2001	Total
748 Biposto Europe 1995	3	844							847
748 Biposto Europe 1996		307	420						727
748 Biposto Europe 1997			199	786					985
748 Biposto Europe 1997 Yellow				44					44
748 Biposto Europe 1998 Red				200	310				510
748 Biposto Europe 1998 Yellow				200	207				407
748 Biposto Europe 1999 Red					532	171			703
748 Biposto Europe 1999 Yellow					341	97			438
748 Economy Europe 2000 Red						430	842		1272
748 Economy Europe 2000 Yellow						223	430		653
748 Economy Europe 2001 Red							786	456	1242
748 Economy Europe 2001 Yellow							386	228	614
748 Economy Europe 2002 Red								244	244
748 Economy Europe 2002 Yellow								52	52
748 Economy Monoposto Europe 2000 Yellow							17		17
748 Biposto California 1997			240						240
748 Biposto USA - California 1999 Red						100			100
748 Biposto USA - California 1999 Yellow					282	28			310
748 Monoposto USA - California 1999 Red						100			100
748 Monoposto USA - California 1999 Yellow					118	72			190
748 Biposto California 1998 Red				90	50				140
748 Biposto California 1998 Yellow				60	150				210
748 Biposto California 1998 Silver				102					102
748 Monoposto California 1998 Red					100				100
748 Monoposto California 1998 Yellow				220	100				320
748 Economy California 2000 Red						80	170		250
748 Economy California 2000 Yellow						170	182		352
748 Economy California 2001 Red							163	119	282
748 Economy California 2001 Yellow							125	210	335
748 Economy California 2002 Red								166	166
748 Economy California 2002 Yellow								170	170
748 Econ. Monoposto California 2000 Yellow						150	50		200
748 Econ. Monoposto California 2000 Red							125		125
748 Econ. Monoposto California 2001 Yellow							75	110	185
748 Econ. Monoposto California 2001 Red							100	75	175
748 Econ. Monoposto California 2002 Yellow								50	50
748 Econ. Monoposto California 2002 Red								50	50
748 Biposto Switzerland 1995		61							61
748 Biposto Switzerland 1996		30							30
748 Biposto Switzerland 1997				40					40
748 Biposto Switzerland 1998					10				10
748 Biposto Switzerland 1999 Red					5	10			15
748 Biposto Switzerland 1999 Yellow					5	5			10
748 Economy Switzerland 2000 Red						5			5
748 Economy Switzerland 2000 Yellow						5	5		10
748 Biposto Australia 1995		20							20

Description	1994	1995	1996	1997	1998	1999	2000	2001	Total
748 Biposto Australia 1996		31	15						46
748 Biposto Australia 1997			25	51					76
748 Biposto Australia 1998				19	4				23
748 Biposto Australia 1999 Red					34				34
748 Biposto Australia 1999 Yellow					10	6			16
748 Economy Australia 2000 Red						33	36		69
748 Economy Australia 2000 Yellow						12	24		36
748 Economy Australia 2001 Red							32	24	56
748 Economy Australia 2001 Yellow							13	17	30
748 Economy Australia 2002 Red								46	46
748 Economy Australia 2002 Yellow								20	20
748 Biposto Japan 1996		10							10
748 Biposto Japan 1998 Red				5	11				16
748 Biposto Japan 1998 Yellow					8				8
748 Monoposto Japan 1998				5					5
748 Economy Japan 2000 Red						32			32
748 Economy Japan 2001 Red							64	5	69
748 Economy Japan 2001 Yellow							40	5	45
748 Economy Japan 2002 Yellow								10	10
748 Econ. Monoposto Japan 2000 Red						28			28
748 Econ. Monoposto Japan 2000 Yellow						12	18		30
748 Econ. Monoposto Japan 2001 Red							40		40
748 Econ. Monoposto Japan 2001 Yellow							30		30
748 Econ. Monoposto Japan 2002 Red								25	25
748 Econ. Monoposto Japan 2002 Yellow								15	15
748 Biposto Germany 1995		210							210
748 Biposto Germany 1996		80	80						160
748 Biposto Germany 1997			60	245					305
748 Biposto Germany 1998 Red					120				120
748 Biposto Germany 1998 Yellow					45				45
748 Biposto England 1995		145							145
748 Biposto England 1996		60	45						105
748 Biposto England 1997			40	220					260
748 Biposto England 1997 Yellow				40					40
748 Biposto England 1998				60	195				255
748 Biposto England 1998 Yellow				41	125				166
748 Biposto England 1999					36	189			225
748 Biposto England 1999 Yellow					45	20			65
748 Economy England 2000 Red						30	150		180
748 Economy England 2000 Yellow						10	75		85
748 Economy England 2001 Red							256	60	316
748 Economy England 2001 Yellow							50	30	80
748 Economy England 2002 Red								60	60
748 Economy England Monoposto 2000 Yellow							15		15
748 S.P. Europe 1995	1	600							601
748 S.P. Europe 1996			400						400
748 S.P. Europe 1997				305					305
748 S.P.S. Europe 1998				88	267				355
748 S.P.S. Europe 1999					152				152
748 S.P.S. Europe 2000						3			3
748 S.P.S. Australia 1998				14	30				44
748 S.P.S. Australia 1999					11				11
748 S.P.S. Japan 1998				28	33				61
748 S.P.S. Japan 1999					18				18
748 S.P.S. Germany 1998				30					30
748 S.P.S. England 1998				40	40				80
748 S.P.S. England 1999					20				20
748 Monoposto France 1995		120							120

Description	1994	1995	1996	1997	1998	1999	2000	2001	Total
748 Monoposto France 1996		40	30						70
748 Monoposto USA 1997			6						6
748 Monoposto California 1997 Yellow				190					190
748 S Monoposto California 2001 Red							75	69	144
748 S Monoposto California 2001 Yellow							125	147	272
748 S Monoposto California 2002 Grey Opaque								200	200
748 S Monoposto Europe 1997 Red				25					25
748 S Monoposto Europe 1997 Yellow				10					10
748 S Monoposto Germany 1997 Red				32					32
748 S Monoposto Germany 1997 Yellow				3					3
748 S Monoposto England 1997 Red				20					20
748 S Monoposto England 1997 Yellow				10					10
748 S Monoposto Europe 2000 Red						2	65		67
748 S Monoposto Europe 2000 Yellow						4	25		29
748 S Monoposto Europe 2001 Red							21		21
748 S Monoposto Europe 2001 Yellow							5		5
748 S Monoposto Japan 2001 Red							20		20
748 S Monoposto Japan 2001 Yellow							30		30
748 S Monoposto Japan 2002 Red								15	15
748 S Monoposto Japan 2002 Yellow								10	10
748 S Monoposto Japan 2002 Grey Opaque								25	25
748 S Monoposto England 2000 Red							20		20
748 S Monoposto England 2000 Yellow							10		10
748 S Europe 2000 Red						3	420		423
748 S Europe 2000 Yellow						1	255		256
748 S Europe 2001 Red							387	40	427
748 S Europe 2001 Yellow							359	40	399
748 S Europe 2002 Red								60	60
748 S Europe 2002 Grey Opaque								116	116
748 S California 2000 Red							200		200
748 S California 2000 Yellow							100		100
748 S California 2001 Red							1		1
748 S Japan 2001 Red							1	5	6
748 S Japan 2001 Yellow								5	5
748 S England 2000 Red							30		30
748 S England 2000 Yellow							45		45
748 S England 2001 Red							65		65
748 S England 2001 Yellow							35		35
748 S England 2002 Red								35	35
748 S England 2002 Yellow								5	5
748 S England 2002 Grey Opaque								30	30
748 R Europe 2000 Yellow						139	551		690
748 R Europe 2001 Red							136	259	395
748 R Europe 2001 Yellow							106	67	173
748 R Europe 2002 Red								177	177
748 R Europe 2002 Yellow								89	89
748 R England 2000 Yellow							150		150
748 R England 2001 Red								60	60
748 R England 2001 Yellow							1	20	21
748 R England 2002 Red								64	64
748 R England 2002 Yellow								15	15
748 R USA 2000 Yellow							70		70
748 R USA 2001 Yellow								100	100
748 R USA 2002 Yellow								15	15
748 R Australia 2000 Yellow							12		12
748 R Australia 2001 Red							15		15
748 R Australia 2001 Yellow							20		20
748 R Australia 2002 Red								10	10

Description	1994	1995	1996	1997	1998	1999	2000	2001	Total
748 R Australia 2002 Yellow								12	12
748 R Japan 2000 Yellow						20	54		74
748 R Japan 2001 Red							12	71	83
748 R Japan 2001 Yellow							14	131	145
748 R Japan 2002 Red								50	50
748 R Japan 2002 Yellow								170	170
748 RACING 1998				20					20
748 RACING 1999					17	1			18
748 RACING 2000						37	15		52
748 RACING 2001							42		42
Model 748	4	2558	1560	3243	3431	2228	7791	4359	25,174

916-996-998

Description	1993	Production at Varese 1994	1995	1996	1997	1998	1999	2000	2001	Total
955 Racing 1995			60							60
955 Racing 1996				31						31
996 Racing 1997					20					20
996 Racing 1998					24					24
916 Monoposto Europe 1994	4	1,443	3	1						1451
916 S.P. 1994/95 alleggerito		310	401							711
916 S 1994 Monoposto Europe		199								199
916 Biposto Europe 1995		9	791							800
916 Biposto Europe 1996			163	550						713
916 Sport Production 1996				497						497
916 Monoposto USA 1994/95		470	323							793
916 Monoposto USA 1996			120	80						200
916 Monoposto California 1994/95		171	89							260
916 Monoposto California 1996			80							80
916 Biposto Switzerland 1994		120								120
916 Biposto Switzerland 1995			220							220
916 Biposto Switzerland 1996			30	70						100
916 Biposto Australia 1994		65								65
916 Biposto Australia 1995			85							85
916 Biposto Australia 1996			50	50						100
916 Biposto Japan 1994		60								60
916 Biposto Japan 1995			68							68
916 Biposto Japan 1996			15	103						118
916 Biposto Germany 1995			340							340
916 Biposto Germany 1996			41	154						195
916 Biposto England 1994		193								193
916 Biposto England 1995			258							258
916 Biposto England 1996			30	128						158
916 Biposto France 1994		141								141
916 Biposto France 1995			360							360
916 Biposto France 1996			40	140						180
916 SENNA Brasile 1995			31							31
916 SENNA Europe 1995		1	149							150
916 SENNA Switzerland 1995			10							10
916 SENNA Japan 1995			35							35
916 SENNA Germany 1995			30							30
916 SENNA England 1995			15							15
916 SENNA France 1995			30							30
916 SENNA Europe 1997					151					151
916 SENNA Switzerland 1997					20					20
916 SENNA Japan 1997					70					70
916 SENNA Germany 1997					30					30

Description	1993	Production at Varese 1994	1995	1996	1997	1998	1999	2000	2001	Total
916 SENNA England 1997					30					30
916 SENNA Europe 1998					56	35				91
916 SENNA Australia 1998					34					34
916 SENNA Japan 1998					41					41
916 SENNA Germany 1998					50					50
916 SENNA England 1998					70	14				84
916 Team Official 1994		14								14
955 Endurance 1995			2							2
916 Factory 1995			6							6
916 Factory 1996				6						6
916 Factory 1997					8					8
916 Factory 1998						18				18
996 Factory 1999							1			1
996 R 1999							6			6
996 R Europe 2001 Testastretta Red internet								2	189	191
996 R Europe 2001 Testastretta Red									120	120
998 R Europe 2002 Testastretta Red internet									5	5
996 RS 1999							11			11
916 S.P.A. 1996					54					54
916 S.P.S. 1997 996 Cc.					4	400				404
916 S.P.S. 1998 Europe						550	408			958
996 S.P.S. 1999 Europe						167	158			325
996 S.P.S. 2 1999 Europe							150			150
996 S.P.S. 2000 Europe							314	261		575
916 S.P.S. 1998 USA						50	50			100
996 S.P.S. 1999 USA Solo							56			56
996 S.P.S. 2000 USA							80			80
996 S.P.S. 1999 Australia							38	13		51
996 S.P.S. 2000 Australia								30	9	39
996 S.P.S. 1999 Japan							72	79		151
996 S.P.S. 2000 Japan								108	40	148
916 S.P.S. 1998 Fogarty Replica England							202			202
996 S.P.S. 1999 England							40			40
996 S.P.S. 2000 England								80		80
996 S.P.S. 1999 France							15	20		35
996 S.P.S. 2000 France								20	30	50
916 Biposto Europe 1997					240	853				1093
916 Biposto Europe 1998						311	634			945
916 Biposto Europe 1998 Yellow						147	245			392
916 Monoposto California 1997					189	111				300
916 Biposto California 1997					34	216				250
916 Monoposto California 1998						100	200			300
916 Monoposto California 1998 Yellow							100			100
916 Biposto California 1998						100				100
916 Biposto California 1998 Yellow							100			100
916 Biposto Switzerland 1997					60	140				200
916 Biposto Switzerland 1998						22	28			50
916 Biposto Switzerland 1998 Yellow							20			20
916 Biposto Australia 1997					80	61				141
916 Biposto Australia 1998						41	45			86
916 Biposto Australia 1998 Yellow							22			22
916 Biposto Japan 1997						25				25
916 Monoposto Japan 1997					45	119				164
916 Biposto Japan 1998							12			12
916 Biposto Japan 1998 Yellow							6			6
916 Monoposto Japan 1998						16	14			30
916 Monoposto Japan 1998 Yellow							15			15

DUCATI 916

Description	1993	Production at Varese 1994	1995	1996	1997	1998	1999	2000	2001	Total
916 Biposto Germany 1997				120	570					690
916 Biposto Germany 1998						205				205
916 Biposto Germany 1998 Yellow						45				45
916 Biposto England 1997				120	460					580
916 Biposto England 1998					114	121				235
916 Biposto England 1998 Yellow					40	101				141
916 Biposto France 1997				140	131					271
916 Monoposto France 1997					100					100
916 Biposto France 1998						80				80
916 Biposto France 1998 Yellow						27				27
916 Monoposto France 1998 Yellow						8				8
996 Biposto Europe 1999						966	898			1864
996 Biposto Europe 1999 Yellow						190	402			592
996 Biposto Europe 2000							1060	706		1766
996 Biposto Europe 2000 Yellow							351	72		423
996 Biposto Europe 2001								715	739	1454
996 Biposto Europe 2001 Yellow								176	145	321
998 Testastretta Biposto Europe Red 2002									559	559
998 Testastretta Biposto Europe Yellow 2002									90	90
996 Monoposto Europe 2000							56	96		152
996 Monoposto Europe 2000 Yellow							18	20		38
996 Monoposto Europe 2001								52	80	132
996 Monoposto Europe 2001 Yellow								16	20	36
998 Testastretta Monoposto Europe Red 2002									57	57
998 Testastretta Monoposto Europe Yellow 2002									11	11
996 Biposto USA - California 1999						303	165			468
996 Biposto USA - California 1999 Yellow						150	50			200
996 Biposto California 2000							302	103		405
996 Biposto California 2000 Yellow							150	208		358
996 Biposto California 2001								250	46	296
996 Biposto California 2001 Yellow								200	101	301
998 Testastretta Biposto California Red 2002									233	233
998 Testastretta Biposto California Yellow 2002									17	17
996 Monoposto California 1999							125			125
996 Monoposto California 1999 Yellow							75			75
996 Monoposto California 2000							120	94		214
996 Monoposto California 2000 Yellow							80	95		175
996 Monoposto California 2001								150	120	270
996 Monoposto California 2001 Yellow								100	75	175
998 Testastretta Monoposto California Red 2002									100	100
998 Testastretta Monoposto California Yellow 2002									75	75
996 R USA 2001 Testastretta Red									60	60
996 S USA 1999 Red						1				1
996 S California 1999 Red						200				200
996 S Europe 2001 Red								136	507	643
996 S Europe 2001 Yellow								37	80	117
998 Testastretta S Europe 2002 Red									163	163
998 Testastretta S Europe 2002 Yellow									1	1
996 S Monoposto Europe 2001 Red								12	308	320
996 S Monoposto Europe 2001 Yellow								1	50	51
998 Testastretta S Monop. Europe 2002 Red									44	44
998 Testastretta S Monop. Europe 2002 Red									17	17
996 S California 2000 Red							200			200
996 S California 2001 Red								180		180
996 S Australia 2001 Red								8	22	30
996 S Australia 2001 Yellow								7	8	15
998 Testastretta S Australia 2002 Red									18	18

Description	1993	Production at Varese 1994	1995	1996	1997	1998	1999	2000	2001	Total
998 Testastretta S Australia 2002 Yellow									5	5
998 Testastretta S Monop. Australia 2002 Red									7	7
996 S Japan 2001 Red									7	7
996 S Japan 2001 Yellow									10	10
996 S Monoposto Japan 2001 Red								25	30	55
996 S Monoposto Japan 2001 Yellow								25	30	55
998 Testastretta S Monop. Japan 2002 Red									51	51
998 Testastretta S Monop. Japan 2002 Yellow									29	29
996 S England 2001 Red								40	180	220
996 S England 2001 Yellow								10	70	80
998 Testastretta S England 2002 Red									46	46
996 Testastretta S England 2002 Yellow									10	10
996 S Monoposto England 2001 Red									15	15
996 S Monoposto England 2001 Yellow									5	5
998 Testastretta S Monop. England 2002 Red									10	10
996 S France 2001 Red									137	137
996 S France 2001 Yellow									11	11
998 Testastretta S France 2002 Red									35	35
998 Testastretta S Monop. France 2002 Red									2	2
996 Biposto Switzerland 1999							60	70		130
996 Biposto Switzerland 1999 Yellow							10	40		50
996 Biposto Switzerland 2000								60	42	102
996 Biposto Australia 1999							96	40		136
996 Biposto Australia 1999 Yellow							22	27	26	75
996 Biposto Australia 2000								40	48	88
996 Biposto Australia 2000 Yellow								10		10
996 Biposto Australia 2001								60	44	104
996 Biposto Australia 2001 Yellow								19	15	34
998 Testastretta Biposto Australia Red 2002									40	40
998 Testastretta Biposto Australia Yellow 2002									5	5
996 R Australia 2001 Testastretta Red									40	40
996 Monoposto Japan 1999							132	32		164
996 Monoposto Japan 1999 Yellow							47	5		52
996 Monoposto Japan 2000								126	50	176
996 Monoposto Japan 2000 Yellow								36	5	41
996 Monoposto Japan 2001									80	80
996 Monoposto Japan 2001 Yellow									50	50
998 Testastretta Monoposto Japan Red 2002									45	45
998 Testastretta Monoposto Japan Yellow 2002									10	10
996 Biposto Japan 2000								14	6	20
996 Biposto Japan 2000 Yellow								6		6
996 Biposto Japan 2001								26	21	47
996 Biposto Japan 2001 Yellow								12	14	26
996 R Japan 2001 Testastretta Red internet									113	113
996 R Japan 2001 Testastretta Red									50	50
996 Biposto Singapore 2000							5			5
996 Biposto Singapore 2000 Yellow							5			5
996 Biposto England 1999							180	342		522
996 Biposto England 1999 Yellow							80	40		120
996 Biposto England 2000								100	115	215
996 Biposto England 2000 Yellow								30	20	50
996 Biposto England 2001									130	130
996 Biposto England 2001 Yellow									30	30
998 Testastretta Biposto England Red 2002									100	100
998 Testastretta Biposto England Yellow 2002									14	14
996 R England 2001 Testastretta Red internet									56	56
996 R England 2001 Testastretta Red									30	30

Description	1993	Production at Varese 1994	1995	1996	1997	1998	1999	2000	2001	Total
996 Monoposto England 2000								20		20
996 Monoposto England 2000 Yellow								20		20
996 Monoposto England 2001									2	2
996 Monoposto England 2001 Yellow									1	1
996 Biposto France 1999						90	135			225
996 Biposto France 1999 Yellow						30	29			59
996 Biposto France 2000							110	160		270
996 Biposto France 2000 Yellow							45	35		80
996 Biposto France 2001								75	97	172
996 Biposto France 2001 Yellow								5	33	38
998 Testastretta Biposto France Red 2002									88	88
996 R France 2001 Testastretta Red internet									13	13
996 R France 2001 Testastretta Red									25	25
996 Factory Replica 1999 Europe Red							100			100
996 Factory Replica 2 2000 Europe Red							147	2		149
996 Factory Replica 1999 France Red							20			20
996 Factory Replica 1999 Japan Red							20			20
996 Factory Replica 1999 Australia Red							10			10
998 Strada 2000							3	8		11
998 Testastretta Bostrom Replica California 2002									155	155
998 Testastretta Bostrom Replica Europe 2002									1	1
Model 916 - 996 - 998	4	3196	3875	2896	5281	5460	6929	5000	5762	38,403

ST4-ST4s

Description	1995	1996	1997	1998	1999	2000	2001	Total
916 ST4 Europe 1996/97 - 1999 Red	3	1	3	365	526			898
916 ST4 Europe 2000 Red					166	327		493
916 ST4 Europe 2001 Red						123	77	200
916 ST4 Europe 2002 Red							98	98
916 ST4 Europe 1999 Grey					19	127		146
916 ST4 Europe 1999 Black					15	84		99
916 ST4 Europe 1999 Blue					256	195		451
916 ST4 Europe 2000 Blue					41	113		154
916 ST4 Europe 2001 Blue						28	89	117
916 ST4 Europe 2002 Blue							16	16
916 ST4 Europe 2000 Yellow					118	73		191
916 ST4 Europe 2001 Yellow						257		257
916 ST4 Europe 2002 Yellow							10	10
916 ST4 USA 1999 Red				428				428
916 ST4 USA 1999 Black				72				72
916 ST4 California 2000 Red					150			150
916 ST4 California 2001 Red						95	61	156
916 ST4 California 2001 Blue						100		100
916 ST4 California 2000 Yellow					99	100		199
916 ST4 California 2001 Yellow						93	60	153
916 ST4 Switzerland 1999 Red					10	10		20
916 ST4 Switzerland 2000 Red					20			20
916 ST4 Switzerland 2000 Blue						5		5
916 ST4 Switzerland 1999 Black					10			10
916 ST4 Switzerland 2000 Yellow					10			10
916 ST4 Australia 1999 Red					66	25		91
916 ST4 Australia 2000 Red					15	13		28
916 ST4 Australia 2001 Red						17	11	28
916 ST4 Australia 2002 Red							10	10
916 ST4 Australia 1999 Grey					13	11		24
916 ST4 Australia 1999 Black					14	14		28

Description	1995	1996	1997	1998	1999	2000	2001	Total
916 ST4 Australia 1999 Blue				7	12			19
916 ST4 Australia 2000 Blue					27			27
916 ST4 Australia 2001 Blue						14		14
916 ST4 Australia 2000 Yellow					17	4		21
916 ST4 Australia 2001 Yellow						15	10	25
916 ST4 Australia 2002 Yellow							2	2
916 ST4 Japan 2000 Red					5	10		15
916 ST4 Japan 2001 Red						28	8	36
916 ST4 Japan 2002 Red							24	24
916 ST4 Japan 2000 Blue					5			5
916 ST4 Japan 2001 Blue						10	3	13
916 ST4 Japan 2002 Blue							10	10
916 ST4 Japan 2000 Yellow						3		3
916 ST4 Japan 2001 Yellow						27	7	34
916 ST4 Japan 2002 Yellow							30	30
916 ST4 Singapore 2000 Red					2			2
916 ST4 Singapore 2000 Blue					3			3
916 ST4 England 1999 Red				60	162			222
916 ST4 England 2000 Red						50		50
916 ST4 England 2001 Red						15	20	35
916 ST4 England 2002 Red							15	15
916 ST4 England 2000 Yellow						20		20
916 ST4 England 2001 Yellow						20	5	25
916 ST4 England 2002 Yellow							5	5
916 ST4 England 1999 Blue				40	45			85
916 ST4 England 2001 Blue						5	5	10
996 ST4 S Europe 2001 Red						2	230	232
996 ST4 S Europe 2002 Red							109	109
996 ST4 S Europe 2001 Yellow							20	20
996 ST4 S Europe 2002 Yellow							38	38
996 ST4 S Europe 2001 Grey Opaque							360	360
996 ST4 S Europe 2002 Grey Opaque							108	108
996 ST4 S California 2002 Red							100	100
996 ST4 S California 2002 Grey Opaque							200	200
996 ST4 S Australia 2001 Red							19	19
996 ST4 S Australia 2002 Red							33	33
996 ST4 S Australia 2001 Yellow							9	9
996 ST4 S Australia 2002 Yellow							15	15
996 ST4 S Australia 2001 Grey Opaque							5	5
996 ST4 S Australia 2002 Grey Opaque							2	2
996 ST4 S Japan 2001 Red							13	13
996 ST4 S Japan 2002 Red							41	41
996 ST4 S Japan 2001 Yellow							17	17
996 ST4 S Japan 2002 Yellow							33	33
996 ST4 S Japan 2001 Grey Opaque							48	48
996 ST4 S Japan 2002 Grey Opaque							96	96
996 ST4 S England 2001 Red							50	50
996 ST4 S England 2002 Red							87	87
996 ST4 S England 2001 Yellow							25	25
996 ST4 S England 2002 Yellow							14	14
996 ST4 S England 2001 Grey Opaque							55	55
996 ST4 S England 2002 Grey Opaque							26	26
996 ST4 S France 2001 Red							22	22
996 ST4 S France 2002 Red							10	10
996 ST4 S France 2002 Yellow							10	10
996 ST4 S France 2001 Grey Opaque							98	98
996 ST4 S France 2002 Grey Opaque							30	30
Model - ST4 - ST4 S	3	1	3	1365	1899	1567	2499	7337

Monster S4

Description	1999	2000	2001	Total
916 HyperMonster 2000	5			5
Monster S4 2001 Europe Red		241	1505	1746
Monster S4 2002 Europe Red			133	133
Monster S4 2001 Europe Black		115	890	1005
Monster S4 2002 Europe Black			11	11
Monster S4 2001 Europe Yellow		85	398	483
Monster S4 2002 Europe Yellow			3	3
Monster S4 2001 Europe CROMO		30	19	49
Monster S4 2001 S Europe Grey Senna		385	1582	1967
Monster S4 2002 Europe Grey Senna			1	1
Monster S4 2001 California Red		52	56	108
Monster S4 2002 California Red			75	75
Monster S4 2002 California Black			75	75
Monster S4 2001 California Yellow		50	50	100
Monster S4 2001 S California Grey Senna		22	178	200
Monster S4 2002 California Grey Senna			150	150
Monster S4 2001 Australia Red		28	30	58
Monster S4 2002 Australia Red			16	16
Monster S4 2001 Australia Black		6	22	28
Monster S4 2002 Australia Black			5	5
Monster S4 2001 Australia Yellow		6	18	24
Monster S4 2001 S Australia Grey Senna			23	23
Monster S4 2002 Australia Grey Senna			26	26
Monster S4 2001 Japan Red		116	134	250
Monster S4 2002 Japan Red			181	181
Monster S4 2001 Japan Black		90	25	115
Monster S4 2002 Japan Black			45	45
Monster S4 2001 Japan Yellow		105	60	165
Monster S4 2002 Japan Yellow			130	130
Monster S4 2001 S Japan Grey Senna			147	147
Monster S4 2002 Japan Grey Senna			144	144
Monster S4 2001 England Red		81	55	136
Monster S4 2002 England Red			44	44
Monster S4 2001 England Black		15	44	59
Monster S4 2002 England Black			10	10
Monster S4 2001 England Yellow		45	18	63
Monster S4 2002 England Yellow			10	10
Monster S4 2001 England CROMO			11	11
Monster S4 2001 S England Grey Senna		20	145	165
Monster S4 2002 England Grey Senna			15	15
Monster S4 2002 Fogarty Europe Red			51	51
Monster S4 2002 Fogarty California Red			100	100
Monster S4 2002 Fogarty Japan Red			35	35
Monster S4 2002 Fogarty England Red			11	11
Monster S4 2002 Fogarty Australia Red			5	5
Model HyperMonster - Monster S4	5	1492	6686	8183

Visit Veloce on the web – www.veloce.co.uk
Details of all books in print • Special offers • New book news • Gift vouchers

186

Also from Veloce Publishing –

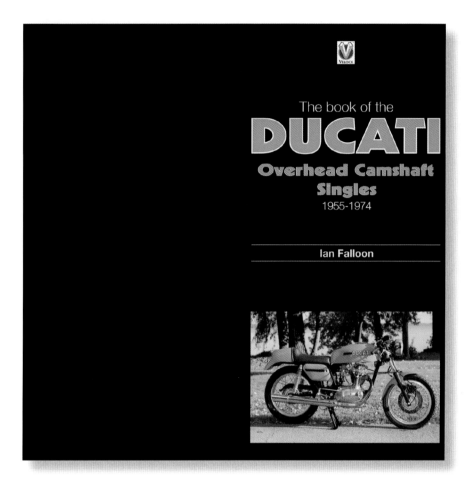

The overhead camshaft single provided the DNA for Ducati motorcycles, but, with little accurate documentation and information available until now, they can be difficult to restore and authenticate. This is the first book to provide an authoritative description of the complete range of Ducati OHC singles.

ISBN: 978-1-845845-66-7
Hardback • 25x25cm • 288 pages • 715 colour pictures

For more information and price details, visit our website at www.veloce.co.uk
• email: info@veloce.co.uk • Tel: +44(0)1305 260068

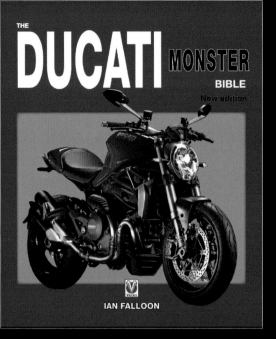

THE DUCATI MONSTER BIBLE
New edition

IAN FALLOON

When Ducati released the Monster in 1993 it created a new niche market for the naked motorcycle that continues today. Continual advancement over the past 18 years has enhanced the Monster's 'less-is-more' philosophy, and Ducati has created Monsters to suit everyone, from entry-level 400s and 600s to Superbike-powered Testastrettas. All Monsters share the naked style that showcases the engine and chassis, while providing ergonomics suitable for cities or canyons.

ISBN: 978-1-845843-21-2
Hardback • 25x20.7cm • 160 pages
• 197 colour pictures

The Essential Buyer's Guide

DUCATI
Bevel Twins
750 GT, Sport & SS, 860 GT, GTE, GTS, 900 SS, GTS, SD, SSD, MHR, S2, Mille – 1971 to 1986

Your marque expert: Ian Falloon

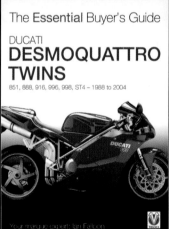

The Essential Buyer's Guide

DUCATI
DESMOQUATTRO TWINS
851, 888, 916, 996, 998, ST4 – 1988 to 2004

Your marque expert: Ian Falloon

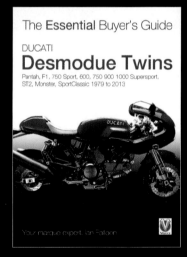

The Essential Buyer's Guide

DUCATI
Desmodue Twins
Pantah, F1, 750 Sport, 600, 750 900 1000 Supersport, ST2, Monster, SportClassic 1979 to 2013

Your marque expert: Ian Falloon

These books' step-by-step expert guidance will help you discover all you need to know about the Ducati you want to buy. Their unique point system will help you to place the bike's value in relation to condition. This is an important investment – don't buy a motorbike without this handy guide – it will help you to find the best bike for your money.

For more information and price details, visit our website at www.veloce.co.uk • email: info@veloce.co.uk
• Tel: +44(0)1305 260068

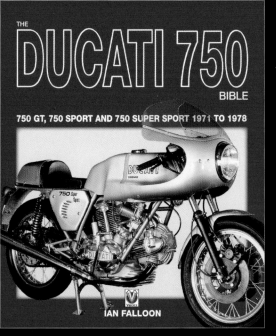

When the great Ducati engineer Fabio Taglioni designed the 750 Ducati in 1970 there was no way he could comprehend how important this model would be. The 750, the Formula 750 racer and the Super Sport became legend: this book celebrates these machines. Year-by-year, model-by-model, change-by-change detail.

ISBN: 978-1-845840-12-9
Hardback • 25x20.7cm • 160 pages
• 163 colour and b&w pictures

This book covers all of the landmark square-case Ducatis of the 1970s and 1980s, including the 900 Super Sport and the Mike Hailwood Replica. Illustrated with 200 pictures, and incorporating complete appendices of technical specifications, this book is a must-have for any lover of fine motorcycles.

ISBN: 978-1-84584-121-8
Hardback • 25x20.7cm • 160 pages
• 178 colour and b&w pictures

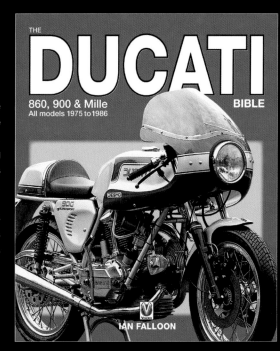

For more information and price details, visit our website at www.veloce.co.uk • email: info@veloce.co.uk
• Tel: +44(0)1305 260068

The book of the
DUCATI
750 SS
'Round-case' 1974

Ian Falloon

Although manufactured for only one year – 1974 – the Ducati 750 Super Sport was immediately touted as a future classic. It was a pioneer motorcycle – expensive and rare, and produced by Ducati's race department to celebrate victory in the 1972 Imola 200 Formula 750 race.
Owing to its uniqueness and rarity, the 750 SS has become extremely valuable and desirable, fetching prices beyond the most expensive contemporary Ducati; for Ducatisti, it is the Holy Grail.

ISBN: 978-1-84584-202-4
Hardback • 25x25cm • 176 pages • 259 colour and b&w pictures

For more information and price details, visit our website at www.veloce.co.uk
• email: info@veloce.co.uk • Tel: +44(0)1305 260068

Index